Home Made Wines and Beers

Home Made
Wines and Beers

Ben Turner

Dedicated to Pauline

First published in Great Britain in 1982 by
the Park Lane Press
This edition published in 1988 by
Treasure Press
59 Grosvenor Street
London W1
This book was designed and produced by
George Rainbird Ltd
Text copyright © Ben Turner 1982
ISBN 1 85051 134 9
Printed in Hong Kong
Printed by Mandarin Offset in Hong Kong

Editor: Fiona Roxburgh
Designer: Gail Engert
Picture researcher: Anne-Marie Ehrlich
Photographs on pages 6 to 13 taken by John Cook of Whitecross Studios

The producers of the book would like to thank Mr Derek Pearman
of W. R. Loftus Ltd, 1–3 Charlotte Street, London W1 who kindly
supplied equipment for the photographs on pages 6 to 13.
W. R. Loftus stocks a comprehensive range of home wine and
beer-making equipment and supplies.

The winemaker and the law

English law at present states: NO WINE MADE AT HOME MAY BE SOLD and NO DISTILLATION CAN TAKE PLACE.

The law in the UK is quite clear. No wines made at home may be sold either privately or to the public. Nor may home-made wines be offered for sale at tombolas, raffles, bazaars, jumble sales, home-produce markets or church fêtes.

If you think that your wine is good enough to be sold, in the UK you must obtain a licence from the Customs and Excise Department and follow its requirements in their entirety. Failure to do so could lead to heavy fines and imprisonment.

HM Customs define wine as any liquid made from grapes, and 'home-made' as that made from fruit and sugar, mixed with any other material which has gone through a process of fermentation.

Winemakers and brewers outside the UK should make themselves familiar with their own national laws.

Notes to the recipes

All recipes for home-made wine make six bottles or 5 litres (1 gallon) unless otherwise stated.

All recipes for home-made beer make sixteen 1-pint bottles unless otherwise stated.

Spoon measures can be bought in imperial and metric sizes to give accurate measurement of small quantities. All spoon measures are level.

All sugar is granulated white unless otherwise stated.

WARNING

When dissolving Campden tablets in citric acid take care to avoid the Sulphur Dioxide which is produced, especially if you suffer from a bronchial condition.

Contents

Preface

This book represents my personal views and comments over a wide range of recipes for home-brewed beverages, from Ginger Beer made for my children, to Blackcurrant Rum which is strictly for adults. They have been developed, tested and varied many times since the summer of 1945 when my great-aunt Jane, then over seventy, first showed me how to make Blackberry Wine. Since then, purpose-made equipment has become available, together with a better understanding of the principles of winemaking. I no longer make single-ingredient, rather sweet wines, but a variety of wines, meads, ciders and beers for different purposes. The table wines are dry and contain a controlled quantity of alcohol appropriate for the type of wine. The dessert wines are very strong and, after long storage, are served in moderation at the end of a meal. Many of the beers, too, I have found to be much improved after three-months' maturation rather than three weeks.

In both wines and beers, experience shows that certain ingredients and methods produce fast-maturing beverages that keep me going until the better brews mature – although, by now, I have acquired a 'cellar' of all sorts.

In the first few pages of this book I explain very briefly, the equipment required and the methods to be followed for making the recipes that are set out month by month in the Calendar. No matter what time of the year you acquire this book, you can begin making wine and beer. There is enough instruction and some simple recipes for you if you are new to 'home brew' and a wealth of new materials and ideas if you have already made a few wines and beers.

Each month begins with a comment on the ingredients available at that time or on what may need doing to achieve the best results. Each recipe is introduced with some personal notes that I hope will help you to share my enthusiasm for it.

A selection of basic wine and beer-making equipment

Introduction

There is good evidence to believe that during 1982 some five million people will make their own wine and brew their own beer – at least occasionally. Most of them continue to do so on a regular basis from 5 litres (1 gallon) a month to 900 litres (200 gallons) a year. For many years I have been making around 370 litres (80 gallons) a year – just under five hundred bottles. When allowance is made for the bottles given to relations and friends, for the extra bottles consumed both formally and informally, I am down to no more than one bottle a day for the whole family. My share averages a couple of glasses – a long way from being or becoming an alcoholic!

A great many people make their wines entirely from cans of concentrated grape juice compounds. They need little equipment, the wines are easy to prepare, and mature quickly. The result is usually entirely satisfactory to the maker and the saving in cost is substantial. Similarly with beer; millions of kits are bought each year and make jolly good beer at a fraction of the cost of the commercial equivalent. Detailed instructions are given with each kit, so no further information will be given about kits in this book.

Having acquired the taste for home-made wine and beer, a great number of people want to experiment with other ingredients and other methods. In the Calendar that follows, recipes are set out that I have made in the appropriate months over the past few years. Most fruits and vegetables can be used in combination to make different wine styles, and several recipes are, therefore, given for the most popular ingredients. Unusual ingredients rarely make a worthwhile wine.

EQUIPMENT

Some basic equipment is essential and it is worthwhile building this up so that you can make some larger quantities from time to time and several wines and beers at the same time. For example, it is worth having three different sizes of **polythene bins**. These come in metricated sizes of 10, 15 and 25 litres capacity – approximately $2\frac{1}{4}$, $3\frac{1}{3}$ and $5\frac{1}{2}$ gallons respectively. Buy those with good-fitting lids and preferably with graduated markings on the side. Make sure that they are of food quality and avoid coloured bins. You will not need them all at first, but eventually you will find good use for more than one. You always need to use a bin larger than the quantity of wine or beer that you wish to make, otherwise you spill the liquid as you move the bin.

Similarly with **demijohns**. These are the one-gallon size glass jars used for the fermenting and storage of wines. Two or three may be enough for a start, but as your stock grows you will need more. **Airlocks**, too, are required, one at first and several later. The glass ones indicate fermentation most satisfactorily but are fragile and easily broken. Each airlock will need a **bored bung** that fits into the neck of the jar. Soften the bung in warm – not hot – water before screwing it on to the end of the airlock, and don't forget to fill the lock with a sulphite solution when you fit the bung into the neck of the jar. **Solid bungs** will be needed for storage but **safety bungs** are worth having if there is a risk of re-fermentation.

How to prepare a yeast starter; the use of a hydrometer in a trial jar

A long-handled **plastic** or **wooden spoon** is needed for stirring and a **nylon bag** is needed for straining out the solids. Several sizes are available in both coarse and fine mesh. A **small press** would be helpful with larger quantities of fruit but is by no means essential.

More important, however, are a **hydrometer** and a **trial jar**. The recipes have been calculated to give the correct alcoholic strength in the finished wines and beers. Nevertheless, it is desirable to check the gravity – i.e. the sugar content – of a must or wort before the addition of extra sugar and the yeast. It is also helpful in checking the final gravity of a wine or beer. Many hydrometers indicate the quantity of alcohol that could be formed by the sugar content indicated if it was all fermented. The joy of making wine or brewing beer is to have them as strong, or as weak, as you want them but do remember the importance of balance and that too much alcohol is as bad as, or worse, than not enough. The hydrometer will help you to make well-balanced wines and beers.

A **siphon** is a 'must'. It is needed to transfer a clear or clearing wine from its sediment into a storage jar or into bottles, without disturbing the sediment. Get one with a J-tube on one end and a small tap on the other. Brewers will also need a **boiling pan**. This can be a very large saucepan, a fish kettle or a preserving pan.

A **brush** to clean bottles and jars after use will be helpful. You will also need **funnels** of varying sizes – a small one for bottles and a larger one for jars. A kitchen **thermometer** will be wanted for checking the temperature of must or wort before adding the yeast. Some **record cards** should be used to keep a note of the ingredients used, the methods followed and the wines and beers made. A card that can be attached to the jars is particularly useful.

Introduction

Proper wine and beer **bottles** are absolutely essential. Previously used bottles should have all labels soaked off, should be thoroughly washed inside and out and then sterilised. New **corks** and **crown caps** should be used for sealing the bottles. A simple **corking tool** for wine bottles and a **crimping tool** for beer bottles will also be needed. Decorative **labels**, **neck bands** and **foil** or **plastic capsules** complete the appearance of wine bottles. Home-brew labels also complete the neat appearance of your beer bottles.

HYGIENE

Although not strictly part of the equipment, it is well worth while keeping a good supply of **Campden tablets** and **citric acid** in stock. Campden tablets are slightly dearer and easier to use than loose **sulphite powder**. They release a known quantity of sulphur dioxide when dissolved and so are more accurate to use. Combined with citric acid they make a formidable bactericide and inhibitor. Four crushed Campden tablets and 5ml (1 teaspoon) of citric acid dissolved in 575ml (1 pint) of cold water make an excellent sterilising solution. Wash every surface that comes into contact with the wine or beer with this solution, especially fermentation bins and jars, bungs, bottles, corks and caps, siphon, hydrometer, trial jar, funnel, straining bag, thermometer – the lot! You cannot be too careful. Do not wash off the sulphite with water, just let it drain. To make a light sulphite solution for wiping fruit, dissolve 1–2 Campden tablets in 5 litres (1 gallon) water. One Campden tablet per 5 litres (1 gallon) of liquid should be added to fruit musts, NOT to beer worts. It inhibits the growth of micro-organisms and prevents oxidation.

How to prevent problems in all home-brew activities
1. Sterilise all equipment just prior to use.
2. Use the best possible ingredients, avoiding everything that is stale or over-ripe.
3. Ferment at the recommended temperatures given in the recipes.
4. Do not leave the solids too long in contact with the must or wort.
5. Siphon the wine or beer from its sediment as soon as fermentation is finished and again when the wine or beer is bright, or nearly so.
6. Store your wines and beers, meads and ciders in a cool dark place for as long as you can before drinking them.

WINEMAKING

Since wine has been made for some 10,000 years it is clearly not very difficult to make. In the last thirty years, however, we have learned how to make good wine more often than in the past. Good hygiene is the first requirement and good ingredients the next.

Before making a wine, decide on the style you want and choose between a dry table wine, sweet white wine, dessert wine, sparkling wine, sherry style or madeira style.

Yeast: Buy and use yeast strains similar to the style of wine you want to make, such as sherry, champagne, burgundy or hock. There is no doubt that used with a sympathetic must, a good wine yeast makes a significant contribution to the taste and quality of a wine.

Most yeasts are now marketed as dried granules and should be re-hydrated before adding them to a must. The latest research indicates that this is best done in a little water at a temperature of 40°C (104°F). The yeast cells soon respond and can be added to the must where they will rapidly begin to ferment the sugar and convert it to alcohol.

Dried yeast does not keep for ever and is best bought in sealed sachets as and when required. It is no economy to buy large quantities at a time, since the yeast will slowly deteriorate when the carton is opened. Keep sachets of yeast in a cool place, the door of a refrigerator for example, until needed.

Yeast needs oxygen in the early stages to enable it to multiply and build up a large-enough colony to ferment out all the sugar in a must. Once developed, however, it converts the sugar into alcohol more effectively if the air supply is cut off. For this reason it is most important always to fit an airlock to a fermenting wine. This keeps out the air and any spoilage micro-organisms that may be in it, but permits the fermentation gas to escape.

Acid: Although the yeast can function well without air it does need both acid and nitrogen to maintain its activity. Acid is the very cornerstone of bouquet and flavour. Without it the wine tastes dull and medicinal. Yeast cells will not remain active in a solution without acid. The best acid to add is citric since this stimulates the fermentation and imparts a freshness to the flavour of the wine. Many fruits contain malic acid and grapes also contain tartaric acid, so a must containing, say, apples or blackberries as well as some sultanas or concentrated grape juice will

Using a filter bag for straining into a demijohn; how to siphon off leaving behind the sediment

contain all three of the major wine acids if citric is added. 5ml (1 teaspoon) of citric acid in 5 litres (1 gallon) of must is the equivalent of one part per thousand. A dry table wine needs about four parts of acid per thousand parts of wine. A sweet dessert wine needs six or seven parts. 250g (9 oz) of sultanas or raisins or concentrated grape juice contains the equivalent acid of one part per thousand. Some fruits, like bananas, dates, elderberries and figs, contain virtually no acid. Others like red- and blackcurrants, raspberries, gooseberries and cooking apples are very high in acid.

Many fruits and vegetables contain matter from which the yeast cells can obtain the nitrogen they need. But the quantities available vary considerably and it is always safest to add up to 5ml (1 teaspoon) per 5 litres (1 gallon) of diammonium phosphate or ammonium sulphate, or a combination of the two.

Fermentation: Experience shows that white wines develop a better bouquet and flavour if the must is fermented at an even temperature of between 13° and 18°C (55° and 64°F). Red wines need a little more warmth, between 20° and 24°C (68° and 75°F) seems to be best for them.

Racking: As soon as fermentation is finished, the young wine is racked from its sediment. Racking is removing the dead yeast cells and decaying fruit pulp from the wine before it can spoil the flavour. This can be seen as a deposit on the bottom of the jar. The best way to get rid of it is to siphon the clearing wine into a sterilised storage jar, leaving the sediment behind to be washed out and discarded.

Topping up: Keep the storage jar topped up with wine of a similar kind if possible. Use any dry white with another dry white for example, but do not add a sweet white to a dry white in case a further fermentation occurs. It is not important, however, to add precisely the same kind, i.e. apple to apple. You can just as well top up apple with gooseberry or rhubarb. Similarly with red wines.

Sherry-style wines should be fermented to their maximum alcohol content by adding the sugar in small doses at intervals of six to eight days. After racking, the wine, unlike all other wines, should be stored in a vessel not quite full, the neck of which has been plugged with cotton wool rather than a bung.

Maturing the young wines: Light wines made from canned fruit, jams and cartons of fruit juice usually mature in three or four months. Most fruit and vegetable wines need much longer. Store them in a cool dark place in bulk for as long as possible and then in bottles for at least some months more. Store them on their sides in a bottle rack or in cartons.

BREWING

Beer has been brewed in the home since the method was first discovered thousands of years ago, so there are few mysteries here. As with wine, quality beers are made from first-class materials and not from slack malt or stale hops. Use a good beer or stout yeast, too, and re-hydrate it before adding it to the wort. Many home-brewers tend to make their beers too strong by adding too much sugar. The maximum amount of sugar used should never exceed half the weight of the malt. Preferably it should be no more than one third or better still one quarter. The sugar is readily converted into alcohol but being thinner than water, too much alcohol tends to make the beer taste thin. So, get the malt/sugar ratio right before you start.

Water: Water plays a significant part in the mashing of malt grains. Hard water produces better bitters and barley wines, whilst soft water produces better brown ales, stout and lagers. Some calcium sulphate is effective in hardening soft water and some sodium chloride is effective in softening hard water. Most home-brew shops sell packets of hardening salts suitable for their area. The quality of the water used is very important in the brewing of good beer. If you have a problem with your beer, it is more likely than not due to the water used. Water that is chlorinated at source should be boiled before use to drive off the chlorine.

Malt: Pale malt grains are the bais for all beers. Crystal, chocolate and black malts vary the flavour, indeed black malt only contributes colour and flavour to a brew. Malt syrups, frequently called malt extract, can now be bought suitably prepared for the brewing of different styles – bitter or stout.

Adjuncts: Don't be afraid to use some adjuncts with your brews, like flaked rice, flaked maize, wheat flakes, torrified barley and so on but do use them sparingly.

Hops: Hops, too, should be used for their different flavours: Goldings for bitter beers, Fuggles for stouts.

Hops are best boiled with the wort for up to 1 hour. The flavour of the finished beer can be varied by:

a saving some of the hops to add for the last 5 or 15 minutes of the boil.

b by adding a different variety of hop for the last part of the boil.

c by saving some of the hops and adding them to the fermenting wort after the second skimming and rousing.

Hop pellets may be used instead of fresh hops. A few drops of hop oil may be used at (c) but not elsewhere.

Boiling and pitching: After the boil leave the hops to settle for about half an hour, then strain them out and press them gently. Stir in the sugar and make up to the required level with cold water. Check the temperature and the specific gravity. Adjust as necessary with more sugar or water. Pitch the yeast when the wort is at no more than 20°C (68°F).

Fermentation: Stir the beer well, cover and leave it for 24 hours. Skim off the dirty froth and wipe away the yeast line around the bin at the surface of the wort. Stir the beer well, cover and leave it for a further 24 hours. Again skim off the dirty froth, wipe away the yeast line and give the brew a good stir. This helps to disperse the fermentation gas and to stimulate the fermentation. Leave the beer covered to ferment out.

Clarification: When the surface of the beer is clear and still, siphon it into sterilised jars, leaving behind the thick paste of dead yeast cells and hop particles. Fit airlocks to the jars and leave them in a cold place for two days while further sediment is deposited. If you feel it necessary to aid clarification, a proprietary brand of finings may be added in the quantity recommended on the packet.

Bottling: Siphon the beer into sterilised beer bottles, leaving a gap of 4 to 5cms ($1\frac{3}{4}$ to 2 in) from the crown cap. Prime with caster sugar, granulated sugar or glucose at the rate of 5ml (1 teaspoon) per 1.25 litres (2 pints). Seal and store for from three weeks to three months.

If you use really good ingredients, ferment at the proper temperature, skim and stir and prime as recommended in each recipe and maintain good hygiene at all times, you will have no problems.

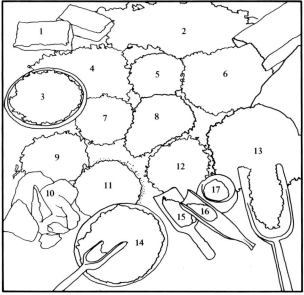

1 Compressed hops
2 Loose hops
3 Flaked barley
4 Flaked maize
5 Crushed black malt
6 Wheat malt grain
7 Crushed pale malt
8 Crushed crystal malt
9 Muscavado sugar
10 Glucose chips
11 Granulated sugar
12 Crushed lager malt
13 Torrified barley
14 Demerara sugar
15 Dried yeast
16 Dried brewing yeast
17 Beer yeast nutrient

January

The new-season citrus fruits have just arrived in the shops and are at their least expensive. Oranges in particular make very good wines. Several recipes therefore include them in both January and February. Parsnips, too, are at their best after a few frosts. Make good use of them either from your garden or the greengrocer. Let me start the year with a few hints that will save you trouble later on.

Don't put your own wine into a bottle that contains the residue of some commercial wine left over from Christmas or from some other occasion when you bought wine. The small quantity left in a large bottle is likely to have become oxidised or even infected by the vinegar bug. It will spoil your wine rather than improve it. Wash and sterilise the bottle before filling it with your own wine.

Don't use old corks, especially those that have been removed with a corkscrew. They will have become porous and even if they do not cause the wine to leak out, they will certainly allow too much air to enter. Your wine may become oxidised or infected. It always pays to use new corks, freshly softened and sterilised.

Don't strain out solids from a wine must or beer wort, stir sugar into a must or wort, rack wine from one jar to another, skim and stir beer, bottle wine or beer, or do anything to expose a brew in a room where there is a strong smell of whatever kind. For example, a room that has been freshly painted or that is being painted; or where onions are being pickled or chutney made. The wine or beer may well pick up the smell and become tainted.

Winter Fun by Frank Dadd, 1893

14

OVERCOME THE RED WINE SHORTAGE

To keep a well-balanced wine cellar it is necessary to make a wide selection of wines for different purposes and occasions. Being a largely meat-eating nation, we really need, therefore, a preponderance of red wines if we are to serve an appropriate wine with our main meal every day. Unfortunately, relatively few of our many fruits make red wine. Blackberries and elderberries do, of course, but these usually have to be gathered from the hedgerow. This necessitates a trip to the country on a fine day, if you can find one when it is convenient to you, during the short season when the fruit is ready for picking. Blackcurrants, damsons and black plums also make red wine but these are often expensive to buy in substantial quantities. All fresh fruits too, need immediate attention, if only in freezing and cleaning them for making into wine at a later date. Sometimes, it seems that the fun of making wine becomes quite hard work! It need not always be so. Home-brew shops sell a wide variety of ingredients to help those pressed for time as well as those a bit short on strength.

Dried elderberries and concentrated elderberry purée can help enormously. All the work of gathering and stripping the elderberries has been done for you when you buy dried elderberries and their flavour is so strong that a few go quite a long way. In that sense they are not expensive. Elderberry purée is even more convenient, since the business of extracting the colour and goodness has already been done for you. One small can is enough to make a dozen bottles of wine. This recipe uses dried elderberries.

250g (9 oz) dried elderberries	*450g (1 lb) demerara sugar*
250g (9 oz) chopped raisins	*15ml (3 teaspoons) citric acid*
4 ripe bananas	*4 litres (7 pints) water*
250g (9 oz) concentrated red grape juice	*Pectic enzyme*
100g (3½ oz) brown honey	*2 Campden tablets*
	Chianti wine yeast and nutrient

Wash the berries in a light sulphite solution, then shake them free of the moisture; you will be surprised at the quantity of dusty particles left behind in the water. Peel and mash the bananas and place them in a large pan with the dried elderberries. Pour on 2.3 litres (4 pints) of water and place the pan on a hot stove. When the temperature of the water reaches 80°C (175°F), lower the heat and keep the temperature steady at this point for 20 minutes. This is a more efficient way of extracting the colour and other constituents than boiling. Less bitterness is extracted and the wine matures more quickly.

Strain out the solids through a nylon sieve or bag, add the washed and chopped raisins to the pan, cover and leave to cool. Add 1.25 litres (2 pints) of cold water, the citric acid, pectic enzyme and 1 crushed Campden tablet. Cover and leave for 24 hours.

Stir in the concentrated grape juice, the honey and the activated yeast. Ferment on the pulp for six days, keeping the raisins submerged. Strain out, press dry and discard the raisins. Stir in the sugar, and when it has dissolved, pour the fermenting must into a sterilised jar, top up with cold water, fit an airlock and ferment to dryness.

Siphon the clearing wine into a storage jar, top up, bung tight, add 1 Campden tablet and store until the wine is bright. Rack again and store for a further nine months before bottling. Keep the bottled wine for some months longer still before serving it free from chill with a pasta dish such as lasagne, canneloni or spaghetti bolognese, not to mention liver and bacon and meat pie.

Should the finished wine taste too dry for you, sweeten each bottle with one or, at the most two, saccharin tablets. These just take the edge off the dryness without affecting the flavour of the wine.

The elderflower

GRAPEFRUIT APERITIF

After a pleasant party the night before, there is nothing like fresh grapefruit to clean your palate the next morning. Serving half a fresh grapefruit for breakfast or sticking tiny spikes into it on which have been impaled pieces of cheese and pineapple, seem to be the two most popular uses of this splendid fruit – at least to many people. Happily, winemakers have an even better use; they turn the juice and very thinly pared skin into an attractive apéritif that makes a welcome change from vermouth.

Grapefruit vary quite a bit in quality and flavour and I prefer the large Israeli variety. Let me hasten to add, not out of any sense of greed for the biggest, but because the fruit inside has a better flavour in my judgement, being a little less sharp and bitter than the smaller Cyprus grapefruit which has a very thick pithy skin that has to be wasted.

To make this apéritif you need to buy your grapefruit in the very peak of condition, while they are really fresh, so choose the best four in the shop. You will also need some ripe bananas to provide the wine with some body but get them very ripe with brown spots on the skins.

4 large fresh grapefruit	*Pectic enzyme*
4 very ripe bananas	*2 Campden tablets*
500g (18 oz) concentrated	*3.5 litres (6 pints) water*
white grape juice	*Madeira yeast and*
1kg (2¼ lb) sugar	*nutrient*

Peel and slice the bananas, place them in a pan with 2.3 litres (4 pints) of water and the very thinly pared rinds of the grapefruit. Bring to the boil and simmer for half an hour, then leave to cool. Meanwhile, squeeze the juice from the grapefruit. Strain it through a nylon sieve to exclude the pips and pith.

Strain the liquid from the pan through a nylon sieve and roll it around but do not squeeze the pulp. Add the grapefruit juice. Stir in the concentrated white grape juice, some pectic enzyme and 1 crushed Campden tablet. Cover and leave for 24 hours.

Meanwhile, activate a Madeira yeast by adding it to 15ml (3 teaspoons) of the concentrated grape juice dissolved in 275ml (½ pint) of tepid boiled water and poured into a sterilised wine bottle. If nutrient salts were not supplied with the yeast, include 2.5ml (½ teaspoon) of ammonium sulphate and one 3mg tablet of vitamin B. Shake the bottle well to ensure a good dispersion, then plug the neck of the bottle with cotton wool and leave it in a warm place. Give it another shake every few hours to encourage the take-up of oxygen from the air to help the yeast multiply. When the yeast is working vigorously, add the starter to the must and make the total up to 4 litres (7 pints). Pour the must into a sterilised fermentation jar, fit an airlock and leave for seven or eight days.

Remove some of the must, stir in approximately half of the sugar and return the sweetened must slowly to the jar to avoid frothing. Replace the airlock and continue fermentation. Five days later, repeat the process with half the remaining sugar and five days later still, add the remaining sugar in the same way. Top up the jar with cold boiled water and ferment to a finish.

When the wine is still and beginning to clear, siphon it into a sterilised jar and add 1 Campden tablet to prevent oxidation. Store this strong, dry wine for nine months in bulk, then bottle it and store it for a further six months.

If the wine is too dry and bitter for your taste, it can be made sweeter by adding one saccharin tablet per bottle of wine. If this is not quite enough, another may be added, but do not overdo the sweetness. This wine is meant to be on the dry side with a slightly bitter flavour. Serve it, nicely chilled, as an apéritif with salted peanuts or crisps.

MOCK MADEIRA DESSERT WINE

Everyone has heard the apocryphal story of how the Duke of Clarence was drowned in a butt of Malmsey wine. It could hardly have been an accident and I suspect foul play. Perhaps some felon stood a butt on end, stove in the top boards and up-ended the poor duke into the wine. Not such a lovely death as might at first be thought. What it does signify however, was the popularity of Malmsey, a type of Madeira wine. A great deal of Madeira was drunk in the nineteenth century, especially by the ladies who enjoyed with it a piece of Victoria sponge cake. It was frequently taken both at 11 in the morning and at 3.30 in the afternoon as well as after dinner in the evening.

For some years now this lovely wine has been out of popular favour and is therefore, frequently neglected by home winemakers. It is however, a deliciously rich and enjoyable wine and the following recipe makes a passable alternative to it.

250g (9 oz) dried rosehip	*2.5ml (½ teaspoon) grape*
shells	*tannin*
4 very ripe bananas	*30ml (1 fl oz) glycerine*
125g (4½ oz) dried figs	*4 litres (7 pints) water*
500g (18 oz) raisins	*Pectic enzyme*
1kg (2¼ lb) soft brown	*2 Campden tablets*
sugar	*Madeira yeast and*
15ml (3 teaspoons) citric	*nutrient*
acid	

Peel and slice the bananas, rinse the dust from the rosehip shells, wash and break up the figs and wash and chop the raisins. Place these ingredients in a large pan with at least half the water. Bring the temperature of the water up to 80°C (175°F) and hold this for 20 minutes.

Empty the contents of the pan into a polythene bin, add the rest of the cold water and when the must is cool, add the acid, 5ml (1 teaspoon) pectic enzyme and 1 crushed Campden tablet. Cover and leave for 24 hours. Stir in the tannin, nutrient and activated yeast, and ferment on the pulp for seven days, pressing the fruit down twice each day.

Strain out, press dry and discard the fruit, stir in half the sugar, pour the must into a fermentation jar, fit an airlock and continue fermentation. One week later, stir in half the remaining sugar and one week later still, the last portion.

When fermentation has finished, siphon the wine into a clean jar, add some wine finings and store it in a cool place for two weeks until the wine falls bright.

Rack again, add 1 Campden tablet, bung tight, label and store the jar in a very warm place, up to 50°C (122°F), for from three to six months to help develop the caramel flavour. The jar should not be quite full. The small air space from the top of the shoulder will also be of use in the development of the

The fig

true Madeira flavour. Return the jar to a cool store for another nine months and then bottle this strong, sweet wine and store for at least a further six months. Serve it cool with Madeira cake at any time of the day.

DRY ORANGE WINE

If you have ever had a winter holiday in any of the countries bordering the Mediterranean, you will have seen oranges ripening on the trees. You may even have had the opportunity of eating one that has been freshly picked and enjoyed the delicious tingle of the cool juice. This freshness and tingle comes across very attractively in a well-made orange wine and January is the time to start.

Just as a commercial wine is often a blend of different varieties of grapes, and cider of different apples, so, too, is a good orange wine a blend of different varieties of oranges. Use some bitter oranges of the sort used for making marmalade as well as some sweet oranges and even a few mandarins.

Only the strained juice and the very thinly pared rind of the fruit is used. The white pith and the segment partitions impart an unpleasantly bitter taste to the wine. The very thin, orange-coloured part of the rind, may be pared with a potato knife or just rubbed thoroughly with half a dozen sugar lumps until the white pith begins to show.

4 bitter oranges (Seville)	3.5 litres (6 pints) water
6 sweet oranges (Navel)	All-purpose wine yeast
2 mandarins	and nutrient
1kg (2¼ lb) sugar	1 Campden tablet
250g (9 oz) concentrated white grape juice or sultanas	

Use the juice of all the fruits but only half the rinds. If you use sultanas, first wash them in hot water to remove the mineral oil with which they are coated. Chop them up, place them in a bin with the peel, fruit juices, sugar and water. Stir well and, when the sugar is dissolved, add the activated yeast. Cover the bin and ferment the must in a warm place for seven days. Press down the floating fruit twice daily.

Strain out and press the fruit, pour the must into a fermentation jar, fit an airlock and ferment out. If the rind is removed with sugar lumps and a concentrated grape juice is used, the must can be poured straight into the fermentation jar.

Siphon the orange wine into a sterilised storage jar, top up and add 1 Campden tablet to inhibit infection and oxidation. As soon as the wine is bright, rack again and store for six months in bulk before bottling and storing for another six months. Serve this dry table wine chilled with roast duck or paté.

SWEET ORANGE WINE

This is another fine wine made from oranges, but the emphasis is on sweetness and a fuller body. The number of bitter oranges to sweet is diminished and some ripe bananas are included to increase the body or fullness of the wine. Use bananas the skins of which are speckled with brown spots since these have a higher sugar content and better flavour.

8 sweet oranges (Navel)
2 bitter oranges (Seville)
2 ripe bananas
500g (18 oz) sultanas or concentrated white grape juice
675g (1½ lb) sugar
4 litres (7 pints) cold water
Pectic enzyme
2 Campden tablets
Sauternes yeast and nutrient
Potassium sorbate

Wipe the oranges over with a clean cloth that has been dipped in a sulphite solution and then pare the skins thinly with a potato knife. Chop up the parings and place them in a sterilised bin with the washed and chopped sultanas or the concentrated grape juice as well as the peeled and sliced bananas. Cut the oranges in half, squeeze out the juice and strain it into the bin, discarding the hulk, pips and tough internal tissues. Save the juice from the last half orange.

Pour on 3 litres (5 pints) of the water and add the pectic enzyme and one crushed Campden tablet. Cover and leave for 24 hours. Meanwhile start the yeast working by adding it to 275ml (½ pint) of tepid boiled water and the juice from the half orange. Stir in 5ml (1 teaspoon) of caster sugar, pour the mixture into a sterilised wine bottle, plug the neck with cotton wool and leave it beside or on top of the bin.

Next day, add the now active yeast to the bin, give it a good stir and replace the lid or fit a sheet of polythene, not too tightly secured with a rubber band or piece of string. Keep the fruit submerged beneath the surface with a weighted plate and leave for five or six days. Strain out and press the fruit dry.

Dissolve all the sugar in the must, then pour it into a fermentation jar, top up, fit an airlock and ferment in an air temperature of around 17°C (63°F).

Check the specific gravity of the must from time to time and when a reading of 1.016 is reached, siphon the wine into a clean jar containing one gram potassium sorbate and 1 crushed Campden tablet. Replace the airlock and move the jar to a cold place to encourage the wine to clear. As soon as the wine is bright, rack again, top up, bung tight, label and store for one year, or longer if you can.

If one bottle of gin is blended with the six bottles of wine at the bottling stage and the wine is sweetened to taste with saccharin at bottling stage, a *de luxe* version can be produced. This really is worth trying sometime.

REAL BEER

After making a few different beers from kits and packs, some amateur brewers like to have a go at the real thing – brewing from grains and hops. It isn't as difficult as you might imagine. Originally ale brewing was part of the housewife's chores. The chauvinist may say 'anything a woman can do I can do better' and most of the amateur brewers that I know are of the male sex. Nevertheless, some women still brew their husband's beer and so for either sex here is a simple but worthwhile recipe to make 14 litres (24 pints).

1kg (2¼ lb) cracked pale malt grains
500g (18 oz) cracked crystal malt grains
250g (9 oz) diastatic malt extract
250g (9 oz) flaked barley
250g (9 oz) flaked wheat (Weatabix)
50g (1¾ oz) Golding hops
5ml (1 teaspoon) hardening salts (if necessary)
9 litres (2 gallons) water
Beer yeast
Finings

Place the malt grains, flakes, malt extract and (in soft water areas) hardening salts, in a polythene bin and pour on 5 litres (1 gallon) of water heated to 76.5°C (170°F), stirring as you do so.

Cover and lag the bin with blankets to retain the heat. Leave for 4 hours, but give the brew a good stir every hour and if the temperature falls to 63.5°C (146°F), add 275ml (½ pint) of boiling water.

Strain out the grains and wash them with 575ml (1 pint) hot water heated to 77°C (170°F), to remove the last traces of sugar. Add the hops, wetting them thoroughly and boil the wort vigorously for 40 minutes in a covered pan. Leave to cool for 20 minutes.

Strain out the hops and rinse them with 275ml (½ pint) of tepid water. Top up with cold water to 14 litres (3 gallons) and when cool, adjust the specific gravity to about 1.038 by adding a little sugar if necessary.

Add an activated beer yeast and ferment at 19°C (66°F). Skim off the dirty yeast head on the second and third days and give the beer a good stir, then leave until fermentation ends with a specific gravity not higher than 1.006. Stir in some beer finings and leave in a cool place for 48 hours or so whilst most of the sediment settles.

Siphon the beer into 24 sterilised beer bottles and prime with caster sugar at the rate of 2.5ml (½ teaspoon) per bottle. Seal each bottle securely and shake it to dissolve the sugar and to ensure that the closure is gas tight.

Store for at least two months, then serve the beer slightly cool, about 15°C (60°F), with crusty bread, cheese and onion.

February

In my early days of making wine I had to adapt other vessels for equipment. A glazed egg crock served as a mashing vessel and ginger beer jars for storage purposes. A small basin or a cup without a handle became an ill-fitting airlock. Looking back I wonder how I did not have one disaster after another. Today there is plenty of purpose-made equipment readily available in all kinds of stores as well as in home-brew centres. The emphasis is on lightness, ease of cleanliness and safety. It is well worth investing in good equipment. It will last for years and the cost spread over the number of bottles is infinitesimal. All metal, apart from stainless steel, is taboo – although unchipped enamel and good-quality aluminium may be used for boiling. Coloured plastic is best avoided too. The natural polythene is quite the best and safest material after glass. Keep your winemaking and brewing equipment separate from that of the household. It is then less likely to become contaminated and impart off-flavours to your beverages.

While the semi-tropical fruits, like bananas, are in excellent supply and often available relatively cheap, it is a good idea to buy them and freeze them against future needs. Purchase very ripe, loose bananas, peel them and lightly mash them with a fork. Mix in a little lemon juice and some sugar, pack the purée into a polythene box, leaving some room for expansion and fit an airtight lid. Label the box and store it in the freezer until it is needed. I keep several such boxes to add to musts that require a little more body.

Oranges may be treated in a similar way. Wipe the oranges over with a cloth that has been soaked in a sulphite solution, very thinly pare the oranges and place the parings in a polythene box, cut the oranges in halves, squeeze the juice and add this to the parings, seal the box, label and store.

It isn't always easy to make wine at the time when the fruit is available and in earlier years when making wine, I often wished I had some other ingredient, particularly those that were quite cheap a few months earlier! Freezing solves many of these problems.

DATE AND LEMON

All through the summer when fresh fruit is in abundance, the natural desire of a winemaker is to produce light table wines. I think it must have something to do with the weather, for conversely during the winter months the desire is to make strong wines. Perhaps that is why Vodka, Aquavit and Schnapps are so popular in countries with really cold winters.

The date has long been a popular fruit for making strong wine. Even today, it is made commercially and distilled into Arrack. Like Calvados, distilled from apple wine, and Slivovitz, distilled from plum wine, Arrack is dynamite to the uninitiated. Dates contain plenty of natural sugar but no acid, hence the combination with lemons. Happily they are both in abundance at this time of year. Using brown sugar with the raisins and dates and storing the wine in a warm place when clear, helps the wine to develop the caramel taste that is so distinctive of Madeira wine. Patience is another ingredient.

2 × 500g (1 lb) packets stoned dates
2 lemons
500g (18 oz) raisins
750g (1 lb 10 oz) brown sugar
10ml (2 teaspoons) tartaric acid
2.5ml ($\frac{1}{2}$ teaspoon) grape tannin
5ml (1 teaspoon) pectic enzyme
1 Campden tablet
3.5 litres (6 pints) water
Madeira wine yeast and nutrient

Doum palms and date palms on the Nile above Philae, Egypt

Chop up the dates and raisins – the big raisins with pips are best, but don't break the pips as they impart an unpleasant flavour. Place them in a mashing bin, together with the very thinly pared rinds of the lemons. Make sure that no white pith is included. Pour boiling water onto the fruit, cover the bin and leave it to cool.

Squeeze out the juice from the lemons and strain it. Add the lemon juice, the tartaric acid, the tannin, the pectic enzyme and 1 crushed Campden tablet to the bin. Cover the bin and leave it in a warm place for 24 hours. Next day, stir in the yeast and nutrient and ferment on the pulp for ten days, pressing down the floating fruit cap twice daily and keeping the bin covered.

Strain out and press the fruit, stir in half the sugar and pour the must into a fermentation jar. Leave room for the remaining sugar. Fit an airlock and leave the jar in a warm place for seven days. Stir in half the remaining sugar and seven days later, the rest.

When fermentation slows right down and finally stops, taste the wine and check the specific gravity with a hydrometer. If the wine does not taste sweet or the specific gravity is less than 1.020, stir in enough sugar to achieve this reading. Move the jar to a cool place and when it begins to clear, siphon it into a clean jar, top up with vodka or another wine. Bung tight, label and store in a cool place.

After two months the wine should be quite bright and must be racked again. Top up, seal and store this strong wine in the airing cupboard or in a similar very warm position for the next six months. Return it to a cool store for a further six months, then it may be bottled and kept for a further six months. Serve it cool with Madeira cake at any time.

PARSNIP AND ORANGE

The abundance of fresh parsnips and oranges, both at the peak of their condition in January and February, is temptation enough to use some of each to make wine. In fact they blend together very well. The parsnips provide body and the oranges flavour. Of course, some grape is included for vinosity and to make good the deficiency in minerals, vitamins and nutrients. This is an excellent combination and highlights the reasons for using a blend of different ingredients. Either dig the parsnips just before they are needed, or buy them from your greengrocer just as they arrive from the market. Top, tail and scrub them spotlessly clean, before cutting them up into dice-sized pieces. Similarly with the Seville oranges, use those that seem the freshest. The recipe includes a sherry-type concentrated grape juice, but an equal quantity of chopped sultanas may be used instead if this is more convenient to you. Although only half a can of concentrate is required, the other half can be safely kept for future use by covering it with a polythene lid, or by transferring it to a smaller, sealable container and storing it in a refrigerator.

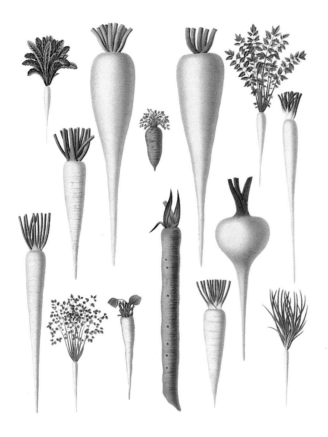

Alternatively you can make a double quantity of this wine, and so use all the concentrate.

2kg (4½ lb) well-frosted fresh parsnips
4 Seville oranges
500g (18 oz) concentrated grape juice (cream-sherry style)
1.25kg (2¾ lb) sugar
5ml (1 teaspoon) citric acid
3.5 litres (6 pints) water
Sherry yeast and nutrient

Clean and dice the parsnips. Thinly pare the oranges and gently boil the parings with the parsnips for 30 minutes in a covered pan, then leave to cool.

Cut the oranges in half, squeeze the juice and strain it. Pour it into a fermentation jar together with the concentrated grape juice. Strain out and discard the parsnips and orange peelings and pour the liquid into the jar. Add an activated sherry yeast, fit an airlock and ferment for one week.

Dissolve the citric acid and sugar in 575ml (1 pint) warm water and boil for 20 minutes, then leave to cool. Add the sugar syrup to the jar and, if needs be, top up with cold water. Replace the airlock and ferment in a warm place. When fermentation appears to be finished, check the specific gravity and if the reading is 1.020 or below, add a little more sugar. Rack into a clean jar, do not top up and make sure that there is an air space above the wine.

Plug the neck of the jar with cotton wool and store the wine for at least one year before bottling. This is a strong, sweet, sherry-style wine.

BARLEY WINE

When it is well made, barley wine is surely one of the great drinks of the world. I have fond memories of one in particular that was out of this world; brilliantly clear, although a very dark brown in colour, a fine malty bouquet, a flavour that was truly a cross between a wine and a beer, a texture that was smooth and a condition that was enjoyably lively.

It is not an easy drink to make and takes at least one full year to mature. The best time to make it is during the quiet week-ends of the winter so that it is ready to drink by the Christmas and New Year ten months and more away. It rewards the trouble taken.

Because it has an alcoholic strength of around 10%, it is wisely served in a 150ml (5 fl oz) goblet rather than a tumbler. This recipe, then, is for just 5 litres (1 gallon) – equivalent to thirty-two servings.

750g (1 lb 10 oz) crushed pale malt
140g (5 oz) crystal malt
30g (1 oz) black malt
30g (1 oz) wheat syrup
30g (1 oz) diastatic malt extract
30g (1 oz) Golding hops
5ml (1 teaspoon) citric acid
2.5ml (½ teaspoon) wine nutrient
5 litres (1 gallon) hard water
5ml (1 teaspoon) Irish Moss
1 sachet champagne wine yeast
brown sugar as required
wine finings

If your tap water is soft, add 2.5ml (½ teaspoon) calcium sulphate and 1.25ml (¼ teaspoon) magnesium sulphate to 5 litres (1 gallon) of water. Mash the malt grains in 3.5 litres (6 pints) of hard water, together with the diastatic malt extract and wheat syrup at a temperature varying between 65 and 67°C (149 and 153°F) for about 4 hours.

Draw off the wort, and rinse the grains with 575ml (1 pint) of hot water. Boil the wort vigorously with the hops and Irish Moss for 40 minutes in a covered pan, then leave to cool for half an hour. Strain out the hops through fine-meshed nylon and rinse them with a little warm water. Add sufficient sugar and cold water to bring the specific gravity up to 1.084 and the quantity up to 4.7 litres (8¼ pints).

When the temperature of the wort is down to 20°C (68°F), stir in the acid, nutrient and an activated champagne wine yeast. Pour the wort into a jar, fit an airlock and ferment in an atmospheric temperature of 16–17°C (61–63°F). Because a wine yeast is used it is unlikely that a normal beer yeast head will appear, although there may be some initial frothing through the airlock. When fermentation is finished, stir in some standard wine finings and move the jar to a cold place for two days for the sediment to settle.

Siphon the barley wine into sixteen half-pint bottles and prime with 20ml (4 teaspoons) glucose dissolved in a little of the beer and distributed evenly among the bottles. Seal each bottle securely and store them for ten to twelve months in a cool place. Cool the bottles and handle them carefully when pouring so as not to disturb the new sediment.

METHEGLIN

Metheglin is probably derived from the Welsh word *meodyglyn*, a medical drink. It was once an almost universal medicine since it contained selected herbs and spices, known or thought to be a cure for different ailments.

The bee has always been thought of as a precious insect, almost sacred, and its products regarded as highly beneficial to mankind. To many people it still is and there is almost a religious cult in the keeping of bees. They have been known to man for some 12,000 years and long before the introduction of agriculture, the growing of vines for wine and barley for beer, honey was diluted, fermented and drunk on all possible occasions.

The medicinal attributes of metheglin, including the aphrodisiac, have now given way to drugs of one kind and another, but the pleasures of drinking it, happily remain with us to gladden our hearts. There are two basic versions of metheglin – one is flavoured with spices (this recipe), the other with herbs.

1.8kg (4 lb) brown honey	Maury yeast
1 large lemon	2.5ml ($\frac{1}{2}$ teaspoon) each of
200g (7 oz) demerara sugar	ground ginger, mace,
20g ($\frac{3}{4}$ oz) citric or tartaric	cinnamon and cloves
or malic acid (or a	1g potassium sorbate
blend of all three)	1 Campden tablet
3.5 litres (6 pints) warm	
water	

Dissolve the honey in the warm water, thinly pare and chop the lemon rind and add this to the honey solution, together with the acid and the spices. Don't overdo the spices. Too little is preferable to too much.

Squeeze the juice from the lemon and strain it. When the must is cool, stir in the lemon juice, the nutrient and an active yeast. Pour it into a jar, fit an airlock and ferment in a warm place for seven days. Remove the lemon parings and stir in the sugar. Replace the airlock and ferment down to a specific gravity of 1.020.

Rack the wine into a sterilised jar and, if possible, filter it, then add 1 crushed Campden tablet and one gram of potassium sorbate to terminate fermentation. Rack again as soon as the metheglin is clear.

It is essential that the metheglin remains sweet since it is not so pleasant when all the sugar has fermented out. Store it for at least one year before bottling, then serve it cool but not cold. Spiced metheglin also tastes especially good when warmed to 60°C (140°F) and served with spicy mince pies.

The herb version is made in a similar way, but a bouquet garni of mint, rosemary, sorrel, balm and mace is suspended on a thread in the fermenting mead for one week or so until just sufficient flavour has been extracted.

GREEN GINGER WINE

This traditional British wine might cause anger to our European partners who have a wine lake for sale, but then they may never have experienced our cold damp foggy nights and the warm and friendly feeling created by Green Ginger Wine. The rich dark colour conjures up thoughts of luscious roots growing in a hot climate. The smooth texture soothes a husky throat, the warmth of the ginger sets us tingling and the alcohol soon has our tongues wagging cheerfully.

Here is a new recipe that produces a super wine for an old-fashioned Christmas. Make it now in readiness for next December.

85g (3 oz) Jamaican root	small pinch of cayenne
ginger (fresh NOT	pepper
dried)	4 litres (7 pints) boiling
500g (18 oz) raisins	water
4 ripe bananas	All-purpose wine
900g (2 lb) light brown	yeast and nutrient
sugar	2 Campden tablets
1 large lemon	Green colouring liquid

Grate the ginger well, wash and chop the raisins, peel and mash the bananas and place all these in a polythene bin together with the cayenne pepper and the thinly pared and chopped lemon skin. Pour the boiling water over them, cover and leave to cool. Squeeze the juice from the lemon and strain it. Add the lemon juice and an activated yeast to the bin, cover and stand it in a warm place for ten days, pressing the fruit cap down twice daily.

Strain out, gently press and discard the solids, stir in the sugar, pour the must into a fermentation jar, fit an airlock, label and continue the fermentation until it stops. Move the jar to a cool place and after three days, siphon the wine into a storage jar. Taste the wine and, if it is not sweet enough, stir in sufficient sugar to your taste. Add 2 crushed Campden tablets and colour the wine to your satisfaction with the green colouring liquid.

Bung tight, label and store for two months, then bottle and keep until Christmas. Serve with hot mince pies. If you think you cannot resist tasting the wine before Christmas, bottle some of the wine in half-size bottles and use these first.

March

When talking with a very experienced winemaker recently, we agreed that every time we made a new wine we put into it all the knowledge, skill and experience that we possessed, firmly believing that this would be a real 'crackerjack' – a *Spitzenwein* as the Germans say. Sometimes our expectations are achieved, but sometimes we fail to reach that peak of perfection for which we had aimed. We are faced with two choices. We can drink the wine as it is, conscious of its lack of character – due most likely to variations in the quality of the different ingredients used – or we can blend the wine with others and fade out the shadows.

Sugar was rationed during the war years from 1939 and did not become freely available until 1952. In that year, having made wine for seven years handicapped by the shortage of sugar, I made wine from every sort of fruit that I was able to obtain.

In the spring of 1953, I tasted my many wines and found that I had a mixed bag of good and indifferent wines. It wasn't that the indifferent wines were bad in any way, it was just that I did not like their flavour. Rather than throw them away and conscious of the thrift imposed upon us by the shortages of the previous fourteen years, I mixed the indifferent wines together, gave them a gentle stir and poured them back into their washed and sterilised jars. I fitted airlocks, just in case the wine started to ferment again and left them for a month or two while they homogenised. They fermented a little, cleared brilliantly and improved dramatically. The wine was bottled, labelled 'Rondo' and greatly enjoyed. I have been blending wines ever since and creating new names for them.

On labels of French wines you will sometimes see the phrase *négociants et éleveurs*, which means brokers and blenders, but never willing to use an ordinary word if a superior description can be found, the French translation of *éleveur* in this context is educator. The *négociants*, or wholesale wine merchants, buy wines in bulk from many sources. Sadly, most of these wines are almost unsaleable at tnat stage. A skilled cellar master tastes the individual wines and with generations of experience, blends the wines together in varying proportions. He 'educates' them, raising them up from their former low quality to acceptable and enjoyable wines. The better qualities of each wine become enhanced and the less desirable characteristics diminish into imperceptibility.

There is great skill in blending and few guide lines. It is mostly a matter of judgement based on experience. There is for the amateur a certain amount of luck and your very first blend could result in a super wine. As a rough rule of thumb, blend opposites: a wine with a very strong flavour with one that is bland and dull; a very sharp-tasting wine with one that is a little insipid. Don't be afraid to experiment, nor to mix more than two wines and even red and white, but do give them some time to interact with each other and become a new wine instead of a cocktail. The chemical interactions do not all happen immediately. Give them at least a month before tasting the wine again.

March

Wines made in the home would improve considerably if everyone concentrated on serving good wine as such, no matter how many different wines were blended to produce it. What is important is the quality of the finished product and not the names of the ingredients from which the wine was made. Try blending some of your wines, now.

I am occasionally asked whether the forced rhubarb available at this time of year is suitable for making wine. The answer is, 'No'. The flavour is so very subtle that the subsequent wine is virtually tasteless. Canned or bottled rhubarb may be used successfully now, but the rhubarb wine enthusiast will wait until the field and garden rhubarb is ready in April, May and early June. Good rhubarb is an excellent additive to many wines.

Rustic Anglers by Charles E. Wilson

340ml (12 fl oz) rosehip syrup
450g (1 lb) redcurrant jelly
250g (9 oz) concentrated rosé grape juice
15ml (3 teaspoons) citric acid
2.5ml ($\frac{1}{2}$ teaspoon) grape tannin
675g (1$\frac{1}{2}$ lb) sugar
3.5 litres (6 pints) warm water
Bordeaux wine yeast and nutrient
Pectic enzyme
2 Campden tablets
6 saccharin tablets

Dissolve the redcurrant jelly in the warm water and when cool, mix in the rosehip syrup, concentrated grape juice, citric acid, pectic enzyme and 1 crushed Campden tablet. Cover and leave for 24 hours. Add the tannin, nutrient and yeast, pour the must into a fermentation jar, fit an airlock and ferment for five days in a warm place. Remove some of the must, stir in the sugar, return to the jar and ferment out.

When fermentation is finished and the wine begins to clear, siphon the new wine into a sterilised storage jar, top up, add 1 Campden tablet, seal and store until the wine is quite bright.

Siphon the wine into the bottles, adding 1 saccharin tablet to each bottle. Keep the wine for a few more weeks before serving it nicely chilled.

This is one of the 'quick' wines and it is ready for drinking in three or four months. Serve it cold at picnics or with ham and cold meat salads.

REDCURRANT AND ROSEHIP ROSÉ

March and April used to be part of the 'closed season' for winemakers in years gone by. Nowadays, wine can be made all the year round from frozen, dried or canned fruit, fruit juices, honey and similar ingredients.

One of the easiest to make during the winter and certainly one of the most pleasant wines to drink during the summer is made from rosehip syrup and redcurrant jelly. Bramble or quince jelly may be used instead of redcurrant jelly. These wines help to promote good health as well as goodwill, since they are especially rich in vitamins.

CARROT AND PARSNIP APERITIF

Winemakers are forever searching for wines that mature quickly. The very best wines cannot be produced in a few weeks since the quality and character of the wine develops slowly during the years of maturation. The different acids, alcohols and tannins, among the 400 identified constituents of wine, interact with oxygen to form new components which in turn interact with each other and so on. This slow process of maturation applies especially to wines high in alcohol such as apéritifs and dessert wines, or wines high in acid or tannin or both. But these wines are very well worth waiting for and every serious winemaker should make at least a few of these wines each year and put them aside for two, three or five years. If they have been properly made, matured and bottled, these wines will keep for fifteen to twenty years and I have tasted some of that age.

This recipe is for such a wine. It makes use of the plentiful supply of carrots and parsnips at low prices, it includes bananas that are currently inexpensive but it does require a few extra chemicals to bring out their flavour. This wine will cost a little more to make than usual, but when mature it will be the equivalent of a wine costing from eight to ten times as much. This recipe makes 12 bottles of wine.

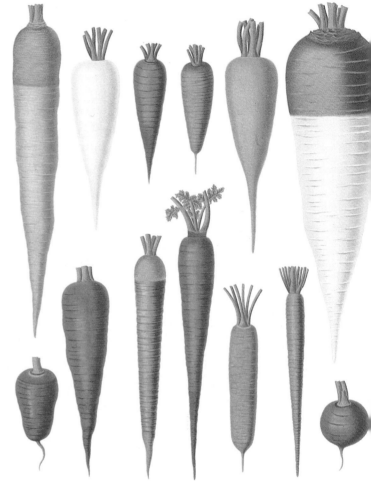

1kg (2¼ lb) concentrated dry sherry-style white grape juice
1kg (2¼ lb) fresh carrots
1kg (2¼ lb) fresh parsnips
8 ripe bananas
2kg (4½ lb) sugar
450g (1 lb) light brown sugar
*10ml (2 teaspoons) each of citric, tartaric and malic acids **or***

30g (1 oz) 'acid blend' (citric, malic and tartaric)
30g (1 oz) gypsum – calcium sulphate
15g (½ oz) cream of tartar
9 litres (2 gallons) water
Sherry flor wine yeast and nutrients

Select the best carrots and parsnips and the ripe bananas. Allow wastage for peeling and trimming the vegetables since the weights recommended are the finished weights.

Activate the sherry yeast in 575ml (1 pint) of tepid boiled water in which has been dissolved 15ml (3 teaspoons) of grape concentrate and 5ml (1 teaspoon) of yeast nutrients. Plug the neck of the bottle with cotton wool and leave it in a warm place. Gently simmer the sugar and citric acid or 10ml (2 teaspoons) acid blend in 2.3 litres (4 pints) of water for 20 minutes, then leave it to cool.

Scrub the carrots and parsnips free from every trace of soil, dice them and boil them gently in 2.3 litres (4 pints) of water together with the peeled and sliced bananas and the tartaric acid or 10ml (2 teaspoons) acid blend until the carrots and parsnips are tender – about half to three quarters of an hour. Leave to cool, then strain into a polythene bin and discard the vegetables and bananas.

Stir in the concentrated grape juice, malic acid or 10ml (2 teaspoons) acid blend, gypsum, cream of tartar, 1.7 litres (3 pints) of cold water and the activated yeast. Cover and ferment in a warm place for four days, then add approximately one quarter of the sugar syrup and continue the fermentation. Repeat this process every four days until all the syrup has been incorporated, top up to the 9-litre (2-gallon) mark and add an extra 150ml (¼ pint) of water to allow for the wastage in racking. Continue the fermentation to dryness.

Rack into a 14-litre (3-gallon) bin or jar, add some proprietary wine finings, cover and leave the wine in a cool place until it is bright, then rack again. Store the wine in a jar no more than threequarters full, plugged with cotton wool instead of a cork. Keep it like this for two years before bottling.

The wine will be a pale gold in colour, with a smell and taste remarkably similar to a dry sherry. Serve it nicely chilled as an apéritif.

WINE FOR DRINKING THIS SUMMER

If we get a warm summer, or even a few hot days in July and August, you will be glad to have some bottles of this delicious wine in the refrigerator. For reasons that we don't fully understand, wines made from fruits that have been canned mature much more quickly than wines made from fresh fruits. The choice is plentiful, but my favourites are gooseberries, apricots and golden plums. You may use any single fruit or even a combination of any two, or even all three in the one wine.

Read the labels on the cans, for some contain 'light syrup', others 'sweetening'. The syrup is normally a sugar base and may be used in the wine. Sweetening, on the other hand, usually implies saccharin and if used will result in a slightly sweet wine. Can sizes vary, but you need to use a total of around 1.5kg (3 lb) of fruit. This would mean three 440-g (15½-oz) tins or a combination achieving a similar quantity. The precise amount is not critical.

Some concentrated white grape juice gives some body and vinosity to the wine as well as amino acids, vitamins and trace minerals to the yeast. The less fruit you use, the more concentrate you need. I like to add around 250g (9 oz) per 5 litres (1 gallon). Again the precise amount is not critical. A pectin-destroying enzyme must be used, some acid, tannin and an All-purpose wine yeast and nutrient. Alternatively, a Hock or Chablis yeast may be used. Pre-activate the variety you use in the usual way.

1.5kg (3 lb) canned fruits	*Pectic enzyme*
250g (9 oz) concentrated white grape juice	*5 litres (1 gallon) water*
675g (1½ lb) sugar	*All-purpose wine yeast and nutrient*
10ml (2 teaspoons) citric acid	*2 Campden tablets*
2.5ml (½ teaspoon) grape tannin	

Open the cans, strain off and save the syrup, mash the fruit with a fork, pour on 2.3 litres (4 pints) water, add the acid, enzyme and 1 crushed Campden tablet. Cover and leave for 24 hours.

Stir in the fruit syrup, the grape concentrate, the tannin and yeast. Replace the cover and ferment for five days, pressing down the floating fruit twice daily. Strain out the fruit through a nylon sieve, stir in the sugar, pour the must into a fermentation jar, top up with cold water, fit an airlock and ferment out in a coolish room temperature, rather than in the airing cupboard or beside the boiler. When fermentation is finished, move the jar to a cooler place such as the larder floor, or outside the backdoor for a few days to encourage the wine to clear.

Siphon the clearing wine into a clean jar, discarding the sediment, add 1 crushed Campden tablet, top up, bung tight, label and store in a cool place for two months. By this time the wine should be star bright, but if it isn't, fine it and one week later bottle it. Keep it only for a few weeks and then serve it well chilled.

This is a light wine in body and texture and has an alcohol content of around 10%. It has a pleasant bouquet and flavour and should be quite dry on the tongue. It is a good thirst-quencher and a delightful companion to the light foods of summer, including salads. Mayonnaise may be served with the salad, but not vinegar which ruins the wine. This is a splendid wine for picnics and barbecues – especially pork sausages and lamb chops, but not steaks nor oniony hamburgers. It is good by itself too, on a warm evening in the garden when you have nothing else to do but enjoy the wine.

Still Life by Edward Laddell

FRUIT JUICES FOR WINE

Grocers and supermarkets always carry a range of fruit juices in waxed cartons, cans or bottles – or all three. Orange and grapefruit are the most popular but pineapple, grape, apple, apricot and passion fruit can be used. Usually these are described as pure, unsweetened fruit juice and they are all excellent for making wine. Some contain a small amount of preservative but this is dissipated in the pouring and stirring process of the preparation of the must. Other juices are pasteurised in order to kill the various micro-organisms that would otherwise spoil them.

But do note that tomato juice does not make a

satisfactory wine and is best served cold and fresh with a dash of Worcestershire sauce.

Interesting and fast-maturing light wines can be made from any of these juices or from any combination of them.

2 litres (3½ pints) fruit juice	5ml (1 teaspoon) pectic enzyme
250g (9 oz) concentrated grape juice	2 Campden tablets
750g (1 lb 10 oz) sugar	German-style wine yeast and nutrient

The method is the same for all fruit-juice wines. Pour the fruit juice and concentrate into a sterilised bin, dilute it with the water, stir in the pectic enzyme and 1 crushed Campden tablet, cover and leave the must in a warm place for 24 hours. During this time the enzyme will dissolve the pectin in the fruit juice and so ensure a clear wine. The sulphur dioxide released from the dissolved Campden tablet will protect the must from infection and any other preservative will have time to dissipate. Keep the bin well-covered to keep out the dust and spoilage organisms that float invisibly in the air.

Next day, stir in the sugar and the activated wine yeast and nutrient, pour the must into a fermentation jar, fit an airlock and ferment out. One of the German-style yeasts is particularly suitable for these wines since the alcohol content required is no more than 10%. The delicate balance is essential.

When fermentation is finished, rack the wine into a clean jar, add 1 Campden tablet and store the wine in a cool place until it is crystal clear. A little wine finings stimulates the clearing process. As soon as the wine is bright, it may be tasted, sweetened with saccharin to suit your palate and bottled.

Made now, this wine will be ready for drinking by the beginning of July. Serve it nicely chilled in a tall, tulip-shaped glass, as a thirst-quencher!

STOUT – THE MAN'S DRINK THAT WOMEN ENJOY

After the barley grains have been malted, they have to be roasted to stop further development. Normally the roasting is just sufficient for the purpose and the result is a pale malt used on its own for making pale ale and with other malts for making other beers. Longer roasting produces a darker malt. Barley grains that are roasted until they are black are included in the making of stout. Water is important, too, because the best-flavoured stout is obtained from soft water. A little table salt improves hard water quite a bit.

There are several variations of stout. One of the best known is 'milk' stout, which contains not milk but lactose, which is milk sugar. 'Milk' stout is,

therefore, sweetish to the taste. Flaked oats are used in the making of 'oatmeal' stout and Russian stout is meant only for strong men.

Stout has been described as 'a domino-black beverage with a glorious creamy head'. It has a dry, bitter taste that pleases many palates, and a body that certainly gives satisfaction. Here is a recipe for a basic stout made from mashing grains and hops. It makes enough to fill sixteen 1-pint bottles.

1.35kg (3 lb) pale malt	40g (1½ oz) Fuggles hops
225g (8 oz) black malt	2.5ml (½ teaspoon) table salt
125g (4 oz) burnt raw barley	9 litres (2 gallons) water
225g (8 oz) brown sugar	Stout yeast and nutrient

Buy the ingredients from your home-brew shop and ask for 'cracked' grains. If they are not 'cracked' you must do this yourself. Soak the grains in warm water for 1 hour to soften them, spread them thinly on a formica surface and roll them with a metal or ceramic roller until each grain is just cracked.

Place the salt and all the grains in a large pan and pour about 7 litres (1½ gallons) of boiling water over them. Check the temperature and adjust it to 65°C (149°F). Cover the pan and insulate it as best you can to maintain an even temperature for 2 hours. A heated serving trolley or airing cupboard do this well.

Strain off the liquid and wash the grains with 1.25 litres (2 pints) of hot water to extract as much of the malt sugar as possible. Add the hops to the liquid and boil them together for 30 minutes, then leave them to cool and encourage the proteins to settle.

Strain the hopped wort into a fermentation bin, wash the hops as you did the grains, and stir in the brown sugar. When the wort is cool, check the specific gravity with a hydrometer and adjust the quantity of wort to 9.5 litres (16½ pints) with cold water and the specific gravity to 1.045. Pitch an active yeast and nutrient and ferment at a room temperature of about 15°C (60°F). Next day, when a dirty scum appears, remove it and give the beer a stir. Skim off the new frothy head on the following day and wipe away the yeast mark around the bin.

After seven days check the specific gravity again and as soon as it falls to 1.000, or just above, rack the beer into a clean vessel and lightly stopper. Leave it in a cool place for three or four days to encourage the sediment to settle. Siphon the beer into sixteen 1-pint beer bottles and prime each one with 2.5ml (½ teaspoon) of granulated or caster sugar.

Tightly crimp on crown caps or screw in stoppers as hard as you can. Shake the bottles gently to dissolve the sugar, then place them in the warmth for seven days while the residual yeast ferments the priming sugar to form a lively condition.

Keep this beer for six to eight weeks in a cool place to mature before drinking.

April

The first piece of scientific equipment that I had to help me make wine was a hydrometer. This simple instrument measures the weight of a liquid against the weight of an equivalent volume of water at a given temperature – usually 15°C (60°F). In winemaking and brewing the increased weight of the must or wort is mainly due to fermentable sugars, although there are some other items present including acids and mineral salts. If you wish, you could always reduce your top reading by from 4 to 6 points to allow for these items. By and large, however, most of the weight is due to sugar and this figure can be increased by adding more sugar or reduced by adding more water.

It is known that a given weight of sugar will produce a fairly precise amount of alcohol. Tables have been worked out to show the approximate quantity of alcohol that can be produced from the complete fermentation of different quantities of sugar. A set of these tables is given on page 79. Thus, by deciding on how much alcohol you would like to produce in a wine, beer, mead or cider and referring to the tables, you can see at a glance just how much sugar you will need in total.

Here is where the hydrometer becomes so useful. It can measure the approximate weight of the sugar already in the brew and by deducting this figure from the total you can quickly calculate how much extra sugar must be added. This easy process enables you to make alcoholic beverages that are not too strong and are, therefore, better balanced. Beverages made in the home are often too strong because an excessive quantity of sugar has been added. Use of the hydrometer prevents this.

Before the yeast is added, strain a sample of the must or wort through a piece of sterilised fine-meshed nylon or linen into a tall trial jar. Carefully place the hydrometer in the sample and when it is floating steadily, note the figure at the level of the liquid. The temperature of the liquid should also be checked since any variation from the norm at which the hydrometer is set necessitates an addition or subtraction to the reading. See the small table following the hydrometer tables on page 79.

Dandelion

THE FIRST OF THE FLOWER WINES

The dandelions will soon be spreading a carpet of gold in the green grass verges. Traditionally you should collect your dandelions on St George's Day, 23 April, but after a long cold winter the crop is sometimes a bit later and lasts some weeks longer. Coltsfoot is a smaller and more refined version of the dandelion but makes a similar wine. Wait for a fine dry day and don't pick the flowers until nearly lunchtime or the early afternoon. By then, any dew will have dried off and the flowers will be fully open. Gather only mature flowers and pick off just the head, leaving all stalk, leaf and grass behind. If you wish, some leaves may be gathered, washed and eaten in salads. They have an attractive bitter taste and are a source of minerals. Select your flowers from areas away from busy roads or dusty tracks so that they are as clean as possible. Place the flowers in a large brown paper bag or a wicker basket, then hurry home and make the wine while the flowers are still fresh. Plastic bags cause 'sweating'.

Remove all the surplus green parts and place the yellow heads in a pint mug or measure. Shake them down but do not press them.

2.3 litres (4 pints) dandelion heads	*675g (1½ lb) sugar*
4 litres (7 pints) hot water	*Sauternes wine yeast and nutrient*
500g (18 oz) chopped sultanas	*25ml (1 fl oz) glycerine*
15ml (3 teaspoons) citric acid crystals	*Wine finings*
	2 Campden tablets

Empty the dandelion heads into a polythene bin, pour hot water over them, add the citric acid crystals, cover the bin and leave to cool. Rub the dandelion heads against the side of the bin with the back of a wooden spoon to squeeze out the fragrant essences from the petals. Repeat this process several times during the next 24 hours. Lift out the flowerheads with a strainer and press dry, then discard.

To the flower water, add the chopped sultanas, nutrient and activated yeast. Cover the bin and ferment the must for five days, keeping the sultanas well submerged in the must. Lift out with a straining spoon and press the sultanas dry, stir in the sugar, pour the must into a fermentation jar, fit an airlock and ferment in a cool place – around 15°C (60°F).

When the specific gravity has fallen to 1.010, rack the wine into a clean jar, add wine finings and 2 crushed Campden tablets. Refit the airlock and move the jar to the coolest place you can find, until the wine is bright and still, in about one week.

Rack the wine into a clean jar, add the glycerine, top up, cork and keep in a very cool place for five or six months. Bottle and keep this wine for a few weeks longer. Serve it cold as an apéritif.

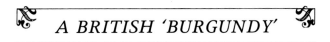

A BRITISH 'BURGUNDY'

The recipe that follows produces a wine similar in style to a *vin ordinaire de Bourgogne* at less than one sixth of the cost. In other words, you can make six bottles of your own for the price of one that you can buy. This wine is so good that the recipe that follows is for fifteen bottles.

250g (9 oz) dried elderberries	*25ml (5 teaspoons) tartaric acid*
250g (9 oz) dried rosehip shells	*5ml (1 teaspoon) pectic enzyme*
125g (4¼ oz) dried figs	*5ml (1 teaspoon) yeast nutrient*
250g (9 oz) dried apricots	
1kg (2¼ lb) Burgundy-style concentrated grape juice	*9 litres (2 gallons) water*
	Burgundy wine yeast
2kg (4¼ lb) sugar	*Campden tablets*

Wash the elderberries, apricots, figs and rosehip shells in clean, cold water to remove the dust. Place them in a large pan with at least 2.3 litres (4 pints) of water, heat them to 80°C (175°F) and maintain this temperature for 20 minutes. Leave them to cool. Strain the liquid into a mashing bin containing the rest of the water, the acid, the pectic enzyme, and 1 Campden tablet. Discard the solids, or make a 'second-run' wine. Cover and leave in a warm place for 24 hours while the enzyme destroys the pectin in the must.

Next day, stir in the concentrated grape juice, and nutrient and an active yeast. Pour the must into a fermentation vessel, fit an airlock, attach a label and ferment for seven days. Remove some of the must, stir in half the sugar, return it to the bin, replace the airlock and continue fermentation. Seven days later repeat the process with the rest of the sugar.

When fermentation has finished, move the wine to a cool place to help it clear, then siphon it into sterilised jars. Add 1 Campden tablet to each 5 litres (1 gallon) of wine, cork and label the jars. Store for two months and rack again if the wine is clear. If not, stir in some wine finings and leave it for one week then rack the clear wine into storage jars.

Store for six months, then bottle and keep it for a further three months. Serve this dry and very enjoyable wine, free from chill with meat or cheese. If you feel that fifteen bottles are not enough, then double the quantities and make thirty bottles, as I did.

POOR MAN'S 'BRANDY'

With so many splendid fruits available I never cease to wonder at the interest winemakers have in potatoes as an ingredient. Perhaps many of us have a little Irish blood in our veins and the interest harks back to our forebears.

This is a very old recipe that I first made more than twenty-five years ago. When I came to taste it the wine was, I thought, a failure and I threw most of it away, saving only one large bottleful to see what would happen. Three years later I knew – it had turned into liquid gold. The colour of gold, it was extremely strong and yet smooth as could be. Indeed it won me my first prize in a show. How I regretted having thrown away the rest. I have learned the hard way that a sound wine that tastes unattractive at the bottling stage should be left alone for a long time to mature fully.

1kg (2¼ lb) old potatoes going soft
500g (18 oz) crushed wheat
1kg (2¼ lb) chopped raisins
1kg (2¼ lb) light brown sugar
2 large lemons
10ml (2 teaspoons) citric acid
2.5ml (½ teaspoon) grape tannin
4 litres (7 pints) water
1 sachet cereal yeast
1 sachet Tokay yeast
5ml (1 teaspoon) nutrient
Wine finings

Scrub the potatoes clean, but do not peel them. Thinly slice or grate them and place them in a polythene bin. Wash the raisins and chop them up, being careful not to break the pips and add them to the potatoes, together with the washed and crushed wheat. Thinly pare the lemons, avoiding all the pith, chop the rind and add to the bin. Pour on 3.5 litres (6 pints) hot water, stir, cover and leave to cool.

Squeeze the juice from the lemons and strain it. Stir in the lemon juice, the citric acid, the grape tannin, the activated cereal yeast, the Tokay yeast, and the nutrient. The cereal yeast will work on the potatoes and wheat and the Tokay yeast will carry the alcohol content to the maximum.

Cover the bin and leave it in a warm place for seven days, stirring gently twice a day to keep the floating cap moist. Strain out all the solids, press and discard them. Stir in half the sugar, pour the must into a fermentation jar, fit an airlock and leave it alone for one week. Remove a quarter of the must, stir in half the remaining sugar and return this to the jar. Replace the airlock and one week later, add the rest of the sugar in the same way then top up with water.

When fermentation finishes stir the wine and move it to a cool place for a few days to begin clearing.

Siphon the wine from its sediment, stir in finings and leave it for two weeks in a cold place. Rack again and store for two years. Bottle and keep for a further year. A long time to wait, but oh! what a smooth, delightful dessert wine. Serve it after a meal.

Wheat by John Linnell Senior

A WINE FOR EASTER

At Eastertide the minds of many people turn to the Holy Land and remember the crucifixion of Christ on the hill just outside the Old City of Jerusalem. By an association of ideas, I also think of figs which thrive in the warm Mediterranean lands. The figs are left on the trees until they drop to the ground, then they are collected and taken into the towns. Deft-fingered women shape and package them and they are exported to many countries including our own. Although they are grown in this country, they are not easy to cultivate. The fig is full of nourishment, rich in sugar, vitamins and mineral salts and it deserves to be much better appreciated than it is. Sadly, it is too often connected with the laxative syrup of figs. Its only concern to the winemaker, however, is its very powerful flavour and only a few figs are needed to make 5 litres (1 gallon) of wine. Like its companion, the date, the fig lacks acid and so combines very well with lemons which are both plentiful and cheap at this time of year. Add some sultanas or raisins for vinosity and you have the making of a fine Easter wine next year.

250g (9 oz) best dried figs	*5ml (1 teaspoon) malic*
500g (18 oz) sultanas or	*acid*
raisins	*Pectic enzyme*
4 litres (7 pints) water	*2 Campden tablets*
2 large or 3 small fresh	*Madeira wine yeast and*
lemons	*nutrient*
750g (1 lb 10 oz) light	
brown sugar	

Break up the figs, chop the sultanas or raisins, pour 2.3 litres (4 pints) boiling water over them and leave to cool. Wipe the lemons with a sulphited cloth, pare them thinly, chop the parings and add them to the figs. Cut the lemons in half, squeeze out the juice and strain it through a nylon sieve onto the figs and other fruit. Add the pectic enzyme and 1 crushed Campden tablet, cover and leave for 24 hours.

Next day, stir in the malic acid, nutrient and activated yeast and ferment on the pulp for four days, keeping the fruit submerged and the bin covered. Strain out and press the pulp dry, stir in the sugar and when it is dissolved, pour the must into a fermentation jar, top up, fit an airlock and ferment out.

When fermentation has finished and the wine begins to clear, rack it into a clean jar, top up, add 1 Campden tablet and store the wine until it is bright. Rack again and store in bulk for six months or so, then bottle it and keep it for a few months longer. The finished wine is not unlike a dryish Madeira wine of the Verdelho style – strongish, well-flavoured and balanced. Serve it cold with strong-flavoured food or even as an apéritif.

The fig is a very useful fruit for winemakers and can be used successfully in combination with parsnips, rosehips, prunes, oranges and so on. It adapts well to sherry-style wines but because of its strong flavour you should never use more than 250g (9 oz) of figs per 5 litres (1 gallon) of wine.

Dried figs make a delicious dessert after they have been soaked in a strong sweet wine for three months. Separate the figs, place them in a suitable jar, pour the wine over them until the jar is full, fit an airtight cover and leave in a cool dark place for three months, giving the jar an occasional shake. Serve them after a meal and drink the nectar afterwards.

RAISIN WINE

It was long before the Pharaohs of Egypt that man discovered that grapes could be dried and preserved for eating out of season. They soon became a commodity of trade and have remained so ever since. They have been imported into this country for nearly 700 years and throughout that time, Cheapside in London has remained the centre of the raisin trade.

Raisins are produced in many parts of the world, but especially in Spain, Australia, South Africa and the United States of America. They are made from black grapes that have been dried in the sun and exposed to sulphur fumes to help preserve them. Some have pips in them, others are seedless. Some

Still Life by Edward Laddell

are from small grapes, others from large. In a good year about three-quarters of their weight consists of fermentable sugars, in a bad year only half and, two-thirds is a reasonable average. This sugar content should not be forgotten when adding raisins to a must. Old recipes for making wine referred to 'Blue raisins of the sun' and this is the kind that I like for this wine: large, blue/black raisins with pips in them. Nevertheless, other varieties make acceptable alternatives and my choice is only a matter of opinion.

1.5kg (3 lb 6 oz) best available raisins	4 litres (7 pints) hot water
500g (18 oz) brown sugar	Madeira wine yeast and nutrient
5ml (1 teaspoon) citric acid	1 Campden tablet
5ml (1 teaspoon) pectic enzyme	

Rinse the raisins quickly in warm water to remove loose particles, then cut them up without breaking the pips. This is something of a sticky job, but it does help in extracting all the sugars, minerals and nutrients.

Place the chopped raisins in a small bin and pour the hot water over them. Cover and, when cool, add the acid, pectic enzyme, yeast and nutrient. Ferment on the pulp for eight to fourteen days, depending on the temperature of the room. Press the floating fruit down into the liquid twice daily and keep the bin closely covered with a lid or sheet of polythene, secured with a rubber band or piece of string.

When the specific gravity of the must falls to 1.010 or just below, or when fermentation appears to have slowed down, strain out and press the raisins dry. Stir in the sugar, pour the must into a sterilised fermentation jar, fit an airlock and ferment out in as warm a place as possible.

Rack the wine into a clean jar, add 1 Campden tablet, top up, bung tight and store until the wine is bright. Rack again and now store the wine in a very warm place (up to 50°C/122°F) for six months to develop the distinctive caramelised flavour of Madeira wine. Then store in a cool place.

This wine should be ready for drinking in about twelve months, but it will keep for much longer. It is quite strong – about 17% alcohol – and dry. Sweeten it if you wish, just before serving it. Served dry and cold, it makes an attractive apéritif before lunch or dinner. When sweetened, it also goes very well with a biscuit or piece of plain sponge cake for elevenses.

The brown sugar, the Madeira yeast and final storage in a very warm place are all important in developing the flavour of this wine. If you want to make it rich as well as sweet, add 10ml (2 teaspoons) of glycerine to each bottle of wine when you sweeten it before serving. Mix them in a decanter and ensure that they are homogenised.

RICE AND RAISIN WINE

One of the most popular wines made by those new to winemaking is rice and raisin wine. The rice contributes body and substance to the wine, whilst the raisins provide that nice grapey flavour. Brown rice is best if you can get it, but I know many winemakers who use the ordinary long grain rice. Sometimes pet food shops stock crushed rice along with crushed wheat and crushed maize. Home-brew shops might also have some crushed rice. If you cannot buy your rice already crushed, then you must crush it yourself. The easiest way is to put it through a food processor or mincer, but failing that, soak it in water for an hour, drain it and crush it on a formica surface with a metal tube or rolling pin.

Sachets of cereal wine yeast are now available from most home-brew shops. They will ferment some of the starch in the rice into alcohol and are superior to other yeasts for this kind of wine.

500g (18 oz) chopped raisins	4 litres (7 pints) water
1 large lemon	1 sachet cereal wine yeast and nutrient
500g (18 oz) crushed rice	1 Campden tablet
1kg (2¼ lb) sugar	

Quickly rinse the raisins in warm water and chop. Seedless raisins can be chopped in a food processor or mincer but not those with seeds in case they get broken. Thinly peel the lemon, discarding all the white pith and squeeze out the juice. Place the crushed rice, chopped raisins, chopped lemon peel and half the sugar in a mashing bin and pour on

4 litres (7 pints) of boiling water. Stir until the sugar is dissolved, then cover and leave it to cool to about 21°C (70°F). Add the strained lemon juice and the contents of the yeast sachet, replace the cover and leave the bin in a warm place for seven days, stirring the must gently each day.

Strain out and press the solids, stir in the rest of the sugar, pour the must into a clean demijohn, top up with cold water, fit an airlock and continue the fermentation. When the bubbles have stopped rising and the wine remains still, siphon the clearing wine into another jar, top up with cold water, add 1 Campden tablet, bung the jar tight, label and store it for six weeks. If the wine is bright, bottle it and keep it for another six weeks before drinking it.

If the wine is hazy, this may be due to unconverted starch. Place a tablespoonful of wine in a white saucer and mix in a few drops of iodine. If the wine darkens or turns blue, the presence of starch is indicated. The remedy is to treat the wine with an enzyme called fungal amylase, obtainable from home-brew shops and chemists. It should be used in accordance with the instructions on the packet.

If the wine is hazy but free from starch, fine it in the usual way and then bottle it from off the sediment that forms within a few days after fining. Add some saccharin to suit your taste.

This wine is best drunk young and chilled. It makes a pleasant social wine to accompany savoury biscuits.

The Young Hop Pickers by William Collins, 1835

INDIA PALE ALE

Although we have not recently been sending beer to India for our troops who were stationed there for many years, the name given to this particular style of beer remains. I must admit that it is one of my favourites. I like my beers to taste of malt and hops, and to have some body and satisfaction. The beer needs storing for at least six weeks and preferably longer to reach its best. That is the sort of time the ships used to take to steam from the United Kingdom to Bombay, followed by a train journey up to the hill stations. Be patient with this beer then. Put it at the back of your store and forget about it for a couple of months. For 16 pints you need:

500g (18 oz) diastatic malt syrup	60g (2 oz) Wye Challenger hops
500g (18 oz) crushed pale malt	5ml (1 teaspoon) Irish Moss
250g (9 oz) crushed crystal malt	9 litres (2 gallons) very hard water
125g (4½ oz) flaked rice	Beer yeast
125g (4½ oz) flaked maize	Glucose chips
125g (4½ oz) torrified barley	Sugar

Using a large polythene bin, dissolve the malt syrup in 3.4 litres (6 pints) of hot water – 75°C (167°F). Stir in the malts, flaked rice, barley and maize. Check the temperature, adding a tiny quantity of boiling water if necessary to achieve 66.5°C (152°F). Cover and insulate the bin. Stir the brew well every half-hour for 3 hours, checking the temperature and adding a little boiling water (if necessary) each time to maintain 66.5°C (152°F). This temperature is quite critical in producing a beer of good quality. Maintain it as best you can.

Strain out the solids through a calico sparging-bag, rinse with 575ml (1 pint) of hot water – 70°C (158°F), add the hops and moss and boil for 1 hour. Leave covered until cool, then strain out and drain the hops.

Adjust the quantity to 9.3 litres (16¼ pints) with cold water and the specific original gravity to around 1.046 (if necessary) with glucose chips or granulated sugar. Ferment under a loose-fitting cover, skim and stir on the second and third days, and then leave to ferment out. Rack into two demijohns, loosely bung and leave in a cold place for a few days while the beer clears.

Siphon into sixteen 1-pint bottles, prime each one with 2.5ml (½ teaspoon) caster sugar, seal, shake and then store in a warm room for one week and a cool store for at least six weeks.

May

Every now and then someone tells me either that a bottle of wine burst and made a terrible mess or that corks go popping right, left and centre. It should never happen, of course. The cause can only be poor attention to fermentation and cellarcraft. Country wines should be fermented in a warm place, i.e. where the temperature is steady at 21°C (70°F) for red wine and a little lower for white. Variations in temperature between a hot day and a cold night, for example, cause irregular fermentation and sometimes fermentation will stick'. A nice steady, even temperature is essential to achieve a complete fermentation.

When fermentation appears to have finished, there is no harm in giving the wine a stir to see whether anything happens. It isn't necessary, but if you are in any doubt, doing this is an extra safeguard. If you have a hydrometer, and every winemaker should have one, then check the specific gravity. A dry wine should show a reading of 0.990 to 0.998.

Remember that it is the sugar which is converted into alcohol and that in the process an equal weight of carbon dioxide gas is produced. This must be allowed to escape and the stirring ensures that none is dissolved in the wine. If the specific gravity is high, say above 1.010, then there may be a cause for danger.

One way to obviate this is to siphon the wine carefully off its sediment, to add some wine finings and 2 crushed Campden tablets per 5 litres (1 gallon), and to move the jar to a cool place for a week. The Campden tablets release the gas called sulphur dioxide which inhibits the yeast and the finings carry the cells down to the bottom of the jar, leaving the wine clean and clear. The wine should again be siphoned off its sediment and then stored for a few months. Some winemakers also filter their wines at this stage so that fermentation cannot possibly begin again.

Safety bungs and stoppers are also available that prevent blown corks or burst bottles. A thin plastic tube is pushed right through the bung or cork and a small portion with an end seal is left exposed at the top. There is a small hole in the side. A rubber sleeve is fitted over the tube and hole. If fermentation recurs and a pressure of gas builds up it can escape through the tube.

After fermentation, all table wines should be given at least 1 Campden tablet per 5 litres (1 gallon) to ensure that it remains stable, to protect it from infection and also from oxidation. Campden tablets are your best friend in preventing problems. Don't be afraid to use them regularly and never forget them.

May Day celebrations in London

HAWTHORN BLOSSOM WINE

Hawthorn blossom wine is certainly a delightful wine. The abundant blossom is a pale pink in the hedgerows in May and later becomes a small red berry about the size of a currant. The wine has all the fragrance and cleanliness of spring and is just as light and tempting. Like other temptations, however, there is a penalty for over-indulgence. A little of what you fancy does you good, so imbibe from a glass rather than from a tumbler. Gather the blossom on a dry sunny day when the florets are fully open. You need enough to fill a pint measure four times. It should be shaken down but not pressed down.

500g (18 oz) sultanas	*4 litres (7 pints) water*
900g (2 lb) sugar	*Hock wine yeast and*
1 orange	* nutrient*
1 lemon	*1 Campden tablet*

Pick out and discard any scraps of leaf or twig from the blossom and place the petals in a large mixing bowl. Pour on 3.4 litres (6 pints) of boiling water, cover and leave to cool. Thinly pare the orange and lemon and squeeze out the juice. Place the rinds and juice in a large pan with the sugar. Add 575ml (1 pint) of water and bring to the boil, stirring until the sugar is dissolved. Simmer for 20 minutes, then cover and leave to cool.

Wash and chop the sultanas and place them in a polythene bin. Strain out the hawthorn blossom and pour the liquid and the strained sugar syrup over the sultanas. Stir in the nutrient and yeast. Cover and leave in a warm place.

Ferment on the pulp for seven to eight days, pressing down the sultanas twice daily. Strain out the fruit, press it dry and discard it. Pour the must into a fermentation jar, top up, fit an airlock and finish the fermentation. Siphon the wine into a sterilised jar, add 1 crushed Campden tablet, top up and store until the wine is bright. Siphon into bottles and keep for at least six to eight months.

Serve the wine cool, fresh and crisp on a warm evening. The wine should be just slightly sweet and if needs be you can sweeten it to your taste with not more than 2 saccharin tablets per bottle of wine.

May

PASSION FRUIT WINE

During the winter of 1976/77 I had the good fortune to spend five weeks in Australia meeting both amateur and commercial winemakers and tasting countless samples of different wines. Four of the white wines stand out in my memory as being quite superb. Two of them were fruit wines and two were made from the Riesling grape. One of the two fruit wines was made from grapefruit, the other from passion fruit. The passion fruit wine had an enormous flowery bouquet, certainly the biggest and possibly the most enjoyable that I have 'nosed' in forty years. The flavour matched the bouquet and was utterly delicious. The wine had been sparkled and was served very cold on a very warm evening. Two of us finished a bottle well within fifteen minutes, a memory that will stay with me while memory lasts – unless the good Lord treats me to another bottle!

Passion fruit of the quality available in Australia is not available in this country, but bottles of passion fruit juice can sometimes be bought in high quality grocers and supermarkets. One bottle – the size varies slightly from brand to brand but the difference is not significant – is enough to flavour 5 litres (1 gallon) of wine. You will also need a little white sugar, enough to make a specific gravity in the gallon of must equal to 1.076.

1 bottle passion fruit juice	5ml (1 teaspoon) citric acid
1kg (2¼ lb) can concentrated Champagne style grape juice	2.6 litres (4½ pints) water
	2 sachets Champagne wine yeast and nutrient
sugar	1 Campden tablet

Pour the passion fruit juice and the concentrated grape juice into a sterilised jar, add sufficient cold water to make up to 5 litres (1 gallon) and check the specific gravity. Adjust with a little more sugar as may be necessary to bring the must to a specific gravity equal to 1.076. Stir in the acid, yeast and nutrient, fit an airlock and leave the jar in an atmospheric temperature of 20°C (68°F) until the fermentation is finished.

Siphon the clearing wine from its sediment into a storage jar, top up and add 1 crushed Campden tablet. Stopper tightly and store until the wine is quite bright. Rack again and store for six months.

Stir in 70g (2½ oz) precisely of caster sugar and the contents of another sachet of Champagne yeast. Fit an airlock and stand the jar in a warm place until fermentation begins. Meanwhile, wash and sterilise six Champagne bottles and hollow-domed plastic stoppers.

As soon as fermentation has started, pour the now cloudy wine into the bottles leaving a 5cm (2 in) headspace. Fit the stoppers and wire them on. Store the bottles on their sides in the warm for five days and then move them to a cold store for at least six months. This period is most important to develop a good bouquet and flavour. Store the bottles on their sides to obtain the best flavour from the yeast.

SPARKLING RHUBARB WINE

There is no doubt that along with elderberries and parsnips, rhubarb has been one of the most popular of country wines for centuries. In spite of this, one often sees references in winemaking books to the danger of using this fruit because the leaves contain a poisonous substance called oxalic acid. The writers usually go on to recommend the removal of the acid with chalk and its replacement with citric acid. It is a case of a little learning is a dangerous thing. The leaves do contain oxalic acid and this is poisonous if consumed. But the stalks contain only a trace of this acid especially during May and early June. The predominent acid is malic – the same as in cooking apples. What is more, the quantity of malic acid is relatively very high, between 1 and 2%, hence the very sharp taste of raw rhubarb. As far as oxalic acid is concerned, there is far more in a dish of strawberries or a serving of spinach than in a dish of stewed rhubarb, let alone a glass of rhubarb wine. Let there be no doubt, then, that the following recipe is good and wholesome.

Pull the rhubarb stalks from your garden in mid-May or early June depending on the season and where you live. Forced rhubarb or late season rhubarb picked during the second half of June or in July is not suitable. The first is flavourless and the second is too bitter.

2kg (4½ lb) freshly picked rhubarb
250g (9 oz) washed and chopped sultanas
800g (1¾ lb) sugar
1 orange

5ml (1 teaspoon) pectic enzyme
2 Campden tablets
4 litres (7 pints) water
Champagne yeast and nutrient

Thinly pare the rind from the orange. Top and tail the rhubarb stalks, removing about 3cm (1 in) from below the leaf and all of the white foot. Wipe the stalks with a clean cloth dipped in sulphite solution and cut them up into thin slices. Place these in a polythene bin with the washed and chopped sultanas and the rind of the orange, you can eat the rest. Pour on the hot water, cover and leave to cool. Add the pectic enzyme and 1 crushed Campden tablet. Leave for 24 hours.

Add the Champagne wine yeast and nutrient and ferment on the pulp for five days, keeping the fruit submerged and the bin covered. Strain out, press dry and discard the pulp, stir in the sugar, pour the must into a sterilised fermentation jar, fit an airlock and ferment out in a coolish position – around 18°C (64°F). Siphon the dry and clearing wine into a sterilised storage jar, add 1 Campden tablet, top up with cold boiled water, bung tight and store until the wine is bright, then rack again.

Keep the wine until it is six months or so old, then remove 575ml (1 pint) of wine, stir in precisely 70g (2½ oz) caster sugar and a fresh Champagne yeast. Return this to the jar, fit an airlock and place the jar in a warm position, 24°C (75°F), for a few hours until fermentation begins.

Meanwhile, wash and sterilise six perfect Champagne bottles and hollow domed plastic stoppers. As soon as the wine begins to ferment, pour it slowly into the bottles, leaving a space of about 5cm (2 in) from the top.

Soften the stoppers in hot water, push them fully home into the bottles, secure them with wire cages and lay them on their sides in a warm place for five days. Remove the bottles to a cool store but keep them on their sides for at least another six months before disgorging the sediment.

RHUBARB AND GRAPE ROSÉ

Country wines are usually made from a single base ingredient with just sugar and water added. The flavour of the fruit predominates. Modern recipes try to increase the vinosity, or wine-like quality, and diminish the strong fruit flavours that are not always to everyone's liking. This is done by reducing the quantity of the main ingredient and making up the body or fullness of the wine with other ingredients, such as dried apricots, sultanas, raisins, bananas and the like. Concentrated grape juice is particularly helpful for this purpose since it is so easy to use. By varying the type of concentrate used, we can vary the type of wine that will be produced.

This recipe is a simple variation on the country-wine recipe for rhubarb wine. There are countless other variations that you can devise for yourself. Bear in mind the acidity of the rhubarb and mix it with other fruits that are less acid to achieve a better balance.

2kg (4½ lb) red-skinned rhubarb
2 ripe bananas
250g (9 oz) concentrated red grape juice
800g (1¾ lb) sugar

3.4 litres (6 pints) water
Pectic enzyme
2 Campden tablets
Bordeaux wine yeast and nutrient
100g (3½ oz) lactose

Top and tail the rhubarb, wipe the stalks clean with a cloth that has been dipped in a light sulphite solution and dice. Peel the bananas and mash them with a fork. Place the fruit in a mashing bin and pour hot, but not boiling water over it. Cover and leave to cool. Add the grape juice, pectic enzyme and 1 crushed Campden tablet, cover and leave for 24 hours.

Stir in an activated yeast and ferment on the pulp for only three days, keeping the fruit submerged and the bin tightly covered. Strain out the fruit through a nylon straining bag and press it lightly. Stir in the sugar, pour the must into a fermentation jar, top up, fit an airlock and ferment to dryness. Rack into a clean jar, add 1 Campden tablet, bung tight and store in a cool place until the wine is clear. Rack again, stir in the lactose and keep the wine for at least a further six months before bottling. Serve this attractive wine nicely chilled with any light food.

⚜ BLACKCURRANT MELOMEL ⚜

Mead was a royal drink whose popularity was greatest in Anglo-Saxon times and in medieval England. Much of the imported wine of that time was probably often somewhat sour and not always pleasing to the English palate. Possibly due to our cold and wet weather, we have always had a liking for sweet foods and drinks. Mead was probably a very sweet drink because there was no understanding of the parts played by acid and nutrient during fermentation. Furthermore the somewhat sweet smell of honey in the bouquet of mead needs to be followed by a somewhat sweet beverage. Even today, a dry mead is something of an acquired taste.

Fruit meads called melomels were once very popular for a change of flavour and are still delicious if finished reasonably sweet. Spiced meads called metheglins were also warm favourites, particularly with the Celts. Served cold and dry they taste horrible in my opinion, but when warmed and sweetened, they really are delicious. I have often spiced, sweetened and heated a mead during one of the cold snaps of winter and always enjoyed it immensely.

I have been making meads since 1954 and have come to the conclusion that, with but few exceptions, most meads taste better slightly sweet rather than dry. One of the exceptions is a dry mead made from orange blossom honey. Meads made from the nectar of flowers share the same need of flower wines to be served slightly sweet. The following simple recipe is for a melomel that will make a delicious and nourishing drink next winter.

one bottle of melomel. To bruise root ginger, soften it in water and when softened use a mallet to bruise a root. Warm slowly while gently stirring in a tablespoonful or two of sugar to suit your taste. Check the temperature of the mull from time to time and remove it from the heat when the thermometer shows the temperature to be 60°C (140°F). Strain out the solids and serve it in warmed glasses. Any left over may be returned to the bottle and warmed again the next day.

1.5kg (3 lb) cheapest blended honey	2.5ml ($\frac{1}{2}$ teaspoon) grape tannin
340ml (12 fl oz) blackcurrant syrup	2.5ml ($\frac{1}{2}$ teaspoon) yeast nutrient
10ml (2 teaspoons) citric acid	All-purpose wine yeast
	1 Campden tablet

Dissolve the honey in some warm water, stir in the blackcurrant syrup, citric acid, tannin, and nutrient. Pour the must into a demijohn and top up with cold water, add the yeast, fit an airlock and ferment in an even temperature around 18 °C (64 °F).

When fermentation is finished, siphon the clearing melomel into a sterile jar, add 1 Campden tablet and store until the melomel is bright.

Taste before bottling and, if necessary, sweeten to suit your palate with saccharin. One tiny tablet dissolved in a bottle of melomel is often quite enough. Keep the melomel until December or January and serve it free from chill.

If you wish to serve it mulled, add the thinly pared rind and juice of half a lemon, six cloves, a piece of bruised root ginger and a small stick of cinnamon to

OATMEAL STOUT

When I was a boy the black bottles of oatmeal stout and milk stout were much more popular than Guinness. It may be that because I was brought up in Kent near three famous breweries: Shepherd & Neame at Faversham, Mackesons at Hythe, and Style & Winch at Maidstone, more of the local beers were drunk. They were certainly very good beers because my maternal grandfather was very fond of them. Indeed, sometimes I had to go down to the Rose and Crown to tell him that dinner was ready and that Nan said if he didn't come at once she wouldn't save any for him! But that was over fifty years ago and local stouts seem out of fashion today.

I say seem, because as a result of the activities of CAMRA, there is a renewed interest in the quality of beer. It depends what you call 'real ale' of course, and I don't like unprimed beers. There is a world of difference between a carbonated beer and a beer primed with a secondary fermentation and adequately matured.

900g (2 lb) malt extract | *40g (1½ oz) Fuggles hops*
(DMS) | *5ml (1 teaspoon) table salt*
125g (4½ oz) black malt | *– in hard water areas*
grains | *only*
350g (12 oz) flaked oats | *9 litres (2 gallons) water*
350g (12 oz) brown sugar | *Stout yeast and nutrient*

Pour 2.3 litres (4 pints) of boiling water into a preserving pan or fish kettle, stir in the malt extract, add the cracked black malt, the oats, hops and salt (in hard water areas only). Boil for 45 minutes with a cover on the pan, then leave to cool.

Strain out the solids and wash them twice, each time with 1.2 litres (2 pints) of hot water. Stir in the sugar, top up with cold water and when the temperature reaches 18°C (64°F), pitch the previously activated stout yeast. Give the wort a thorough stir and cover the bin. On the second and third days skim off the dirty froth, wipe away the dirty yeast ring around the bin and give the beer a good stir.

When fermentation is finished, siphon the clearing beer into glass jars and leave these in the cool for 48 hours while more sediment is deposited. Taste the stout and if necessary sweeten it to your taste with saccharin or lactose – not sugar. Siphon the beer into sixteen one-pint bottles to within 5cm (2 in) from the top.

Dissolve 40g (1½ oz) caster sugar in a little warm water and distribute this evenly between the bottles. Screw down clean stoppers with good rubber rings or very tightly crimp on crown caps. Give the bottles a shake to test the seal, then stand them in a warm place for one week before storing them for another six. You will then agree that this is 'real' beer.

ALE FOR ALL

There are occasions when there is nothing more satisfying than a long glass of cool beer; tangy, thirst-quenching, bitter beer. I made my first beer as far back as 1952 from a very easy recipe that has never failed to produce good results. It has few ingredients and they can be marginally varied in quantity to suit your taste. The beer is simple to brew, matures quickly and is very satisfying to drink.

900g (2 lb) malt extract | *Beer yeast*
50g (1¼ oz) Golding hops | *50g (1¾ oz) caster sugar*
350g (12 oz) sugar | *for priming*
8 litres (14 pints) water

Place all but a handful of the hops in a large pan, add 1.2 litres (2 pints) of water and squeeze the hops in your hand until they are thoroughly wet. Hops have a certain oiliness and float on the surface of the water unless you do this. Place a cover on the pan and boil vigorously for 15 minutes.

Meanwhile, pour 575ml (1 pint) of warm water into a brewing bin and stir into it the malt extract and sugar. A trace of malt may be left in the jar and dissolved in a cup of tepid water. The yeast should then be added to this thin malt solution to become activated. Cover and leave it until required.

Strain the hop water into the brewing bin, add another 1.2 litres (2 pints) of water to the hops and boil them for a further 15 minutes. Again, strain the liquid into the bin, add another 1.2 litres (2 pints) of water to the hops and boil again for a final 15 minutes. Strain the liquid into the brewing bin and discard the hops.

Top up the bin with cold water to the 9-litre (16-pint) mark and when the temperature of the wort has fallen to 21°C (70°F), pitch the activated yeast. Cover the bin and leave for 24 hours, then skim off the dirty froth. Stir the wort well, cover and leave for another 24 hours. Skim off the new froth and add the handful of hops saved from the outset. Wet them thoroughly in the wort, replace the cover and leave for three days, pressing the hops below the surface twice daily.

Siphon the clearing beer into a jar, fit an airlock and leave it in a cool place for three days while the beer clears and throws a fairly heavy sediment. Rack the now just hazy beer into a clean jar, stir in the caster sugar and as soon as it is completely dissolved, siphon the beer into sterilised beer bottles. Fill each one, leaving a gap of 5cm (2 in) from the top and tightly crimp on new and sterilized crown caps, or tightly screw in stoppers with good rubber washers.

Leave the bottles in a warm room for one week, then move them to a cool store for another two weeks, by which time the beer is ready to drink. Serve it cool and pour carefully so as not to disturb the sediment.

June

During a recent phone-in programme on the radio, a listener took me to task for including several different fruits and other ingredients in my recipes. He held the 'old-school' view that wine should be made from a single ingredient with water, sugar and yeast. These old recipes certainly produce sweet-flavoured beverages containing some alcohol and are very pleasant to taste. Indeed, I began my own winemaking that way with blackberries in 1945. Study, research and experience shows, however, that better wines can be made by preparing a balanced must that will produce wines that have fermented out to dryness and possess a complex bouquet and flavour and some body.

The flavour of some fruits is so strong that a sufficient quantity to make other than a very thin wine will produce an overpowering fruit flavour. This is where the odd banana or two can be used. Without changing the flavour it can add a little body. So too, with sultanas, raisins and concentrated grape juice.

The aim of the amateur winemaker is to make fine examples of the different wine styles with vinous and subtle fruit flavour. The pectic enzyme helps in juice extraction and clarity; tannin helps to produce character while acid is the very cornerstone of bouquet and flavour and must never be omitted. Every ingredient in these recipes has a part to play.

The Hayfield by Myles Birket Foster

FRONTINIAC WINE

Many of our old wine recipes included the ingredient 'blue raisins of the sun'. This is such a recipe and I have used the large blue-black muscatel raisins that have such a magnificent flavour. So many other raisins seem to lack depth of colour. This recipe is my version of one that was popular in the eighteenth century. Frontignan is the name of a village in the south of France famous for its dessert wine made from the muscatel grape.

1.35kg (3 lb) 'blue raisins of the sun'	1 large lemon
4 litres (7 pints) water	5ml (1 teaspoon) pectic enzyme
275ml ($\frac{1}{2}$ pint) freshly picked elderflowers	1 Campden tablet
500g (18 oz) sugar	Tokay yeast and nutrient

Wash and chop the raisins, being careful not to break any pips. Pour cold water over them. Thinly pare the lemon, chop the peel and squeeze the juice; add the parings and strained juice to the raisins. Add the pectic enzyme and 1 crushed Campden tablet, cover and leave for 24 hours. Add the elderflowers, freshly shaken from their stalks and from which every piece of green stem has been discarded.

Stir in a rehydrated yeast and nutrient and ferment on the pulp, keeping the cap pressed down and the container covered. After ten days, strain out and press the pulp dry before discarding it. Stir in half the sugar, pour the must into a demijohn, fit an airlock and continue the fermentation. After five days, stir in half the remaining sugar, and five days later, the rest.

When fermentation finishes, siphon the clearing wine into a storage jar, top up, seal tight and store until the wine is bright. Rack again and keep the wine in store for one year before bottling it. Serve it chilled with shortbread.

ELDERFLOWER – THE QUEEN OF THE WINES

Two hundred years ago and more, country folk in their cottages made many wines to promote or restore health. But at this time of the year they made elderflower wine for the sheer pleasure of drinking it. The tradition has continued and people still eulogise about this flower wine, more than any other. The fragrance of the florets when picking them is reminiscent of bananas – warm and smooth and soft – but there are several varieties of the elder tree and some have what has been described as a 'catty' smell. Watch out for these and leave them alone. Sadly, the flower has only bouquet and flavour to give the wine and it would be a pity to use other than the most attractive variety. The wine should not be too strong. The golden 'robe' should cover a light and supple 'body' and the 'farewell' should linger longingly on the palate.

Gather the florets on a warm dry afternoon when they are fully open. Place them in a paper bag rather than a plastic one that causes 'sweating'. Gather them thoughtfully, being careful not to damage the tree, nor to take all the florets, leaving some to form the berries for our winter winemaking. For 5 litres (1 gallon) of wine, you need only 575ml (1 pint) of elderflowers, so there is no need to be greedy.

As soon as you get home, pick the florets from their green stems and discard these with all the stalks and leaves since they impart a bitter taste to the wine. Measure the florets in a jug and shake them down by banging the jug gently on the table; don't press them down. There are two ways of making this wine.

Recipe A

575ml (1 pint) cleaned elderflower florets	3.5 litres (6 pints) hot water
1kg ($2\frac{1}{4}$ lb) Sauternes-style concentrated grape juice	All-purpose wine yeast and nutrient
275g (10 oz) sugar	Campden tablets

Place the cleaned elderflowers in a ceramic bowl and pour the hot water over them. Rub the petals against the side of the bowl with the back of wooden spoon to extract the fragrance. Cover and leave to cool. Repeat the maceration of the petals several times during the following 24 hours. Strain out the petals, press them dry and discard them. Use the flavoured water with the concentrated grape juice to make the wine in accordance with the instructions given on the can.

Recipe B

575ml (1 pint) cleaned elderflower florets	4.3 litres ($7\frac{1}{2}$ pints) hot water
900g (2 lb) sultanas	All-purpose wine yeast and nutrient
5ml (1 teaspoon) citric acid	Potassium sorbate
350g (12 oz) sugar	1 Campden tablet

Place the cleaned elderflowers in a polythene bin and pour the hot water over them. Rub the petals against the side of the bin with the back of a wooden spoon to extract the fragrance. Add the washed and chopped sultanas and the citric acid, stir well, cover and leave to cool. Mix in the yeast and nutrient and ferment on the pulp for ten days, keeping the fruit submerged and the container covered.

Strain out and press the pulp dry, stir in the sugar, pour the must into a demijohn, top up, fit an airlock and ferment down to a specific gravity of 1.006.

Rack into a clean jar, add one gram of potassium sorbate and 1 crushed Campden tablet to terminate fermentation. Top up, bung tight, label and store in a cold place until the wine is bright, then rack again. Keep the wine in bulk for six months, then bottle and keep it for a further three months.

Serve it cold with sweet biscuits.

A medieval lady gathering parsley in her herb garden

PARSLEY WINE

Most wine drinkers are well aware of the dictum to drink white wine with fish. Happily we have a great range of suitable wines for the purpose. But even among white wines some are more suitable than others. Among the great range of commercial white wines, Muscadet, for example, makes the best accompaniment to all shellfish and to many others as well.

In the same way, parsley wine makes the best white country wine to accompany fish. Perhaps it is the herbal quality of the parsley that adds to the piquancy of this wine. It is certainly a wine to make if you have access to a good quantity of fresh parsley. Towards the end of June is the best time to pick the fresh, green, crinkled leaves. Gather them in the early morning before the hot sun has started to dry them and leaves them drooping and wilting. Cut off any superfluous stems and weigh the young and tender leaves.

450g (1 lb) fresh parsley	*900g (2 lb) white sugar*
500g (18 oz) sultanas	*4 litres (7 pints) water*
2 fresh lemons	*Hock yeast and nutrient*
2 fresh oranges	*1 Campden tablet*

Coarsely chop the parsley, place it in a bin and pour boiling water over it, cover and leave for 24 hours. Pare the oranges and lemons and express the juice. Discard all the pith. Strain out the parsley, add the chopped sultanas, the thinly pared orange and lemon skins, the juice, and half the sugar to the bin. Stir the must well and when the sugar is dissolved, add an active yeast and nutrient.

Cover the bin and ferment for five days keeping the sultanas and fruit skins submerged. Strain out and press these solids, stir in the rest of the sugar, pour the fermenting must into a demijohn, top up with cold water, fit an airlock and ferment to dryness. Move the jar to a cool place for a few days, then siphon the clearing wine into a clean jar. Add 1 Campden tablet and store the wine until it is bright, then rack again. When the wine is about four months old, bottle it and keep it for a further two or three months.

Serve this wine nicely chilled with any fish dish, other than fried fish and chips.

RED ROSES FOR WINE

No wonder England chose the rose for its emblem. Apart from flourishing on our beastly clay, an established bush will produce three crops of flowers in a season. But the spent flowers do not have to be thrown away like other flowers, they can be made into a wondrous wine. The deep red petals from such varieties as Wendy Cousins, Josephine Bruce, Fragrant Cloud, Madame Lapèrière and Super Star are among the most suitable for making wine. All are heavily scented.

When the rose is 'blown' but just before 'petal fall' is the best time to gather the petals. Make sure that you do not include the seed box nor any leaves. You need a 1.2-litre (2-pint) measure of petals pressed lightly down to make 5 litres (1 gallon) of wine. The liquid contains only colour and perfume, so other ingredients must be added to make the wine. Traditionally sultanas were used but a concentrated grape juice is even better. Use a rosé rather than a red grape juice. If a rosé is not available use a sweet white grape juice.

1.2 litres (2 pints) rose	*675g (1½ lb) sugar*
petals	*10ml (2 teaspoons)*
500g (18 oz) sultanas **or**	*tartaric acid*
500g (18 oz) concentrated	*2 Campden tablets*
rose grape juice	*1 sachet Sauternes yeast*

Place the petals in a ceramic mixing bowl, pour boiling water over them and macerate them gently with the back of a wooden spoon. Cover them and leave them for three days, rubbing the petals with the back of the spoon twice each day to extract all the perfume.

Keep the bowl well covered in the meantime, then strain off the liquid and press the petals. If using sultanas rather than concentrated grape juice, wash and chop them. Mix all the ingredients together and make up to 5 litres (1 gallon). Pour the must into a fermentation jar, fit an airlock and leave the jar in a warm place for two or three weeks. Keep an eye on the descending specific gravity. Rose petal wine is essentially a sweetish wine and the gravity should not be allowed to fall much below 1.010. At this point, or even a little above, rack the wine into a clean jar containing 2 crushed Campden tablets to terminate fermentation. Move the jar to a cool place to encourage the wine to clear naturally.

As soon as the wine is bright, siphon it into bottles, cork and label them and place them in a cool store for about six months. Serve the wine cool at 12°C (54°F) with a piece of Victoria sandwich or a shortbread biscuit. You will find it lovely to look at, exciting to smell and heavenly to taste.

NETTLE BEER

An elderly lady once asked me for a recipe for nettle beer. She remembered her grandmother making it when she was a child, but had long since lost the recipe. Nettles were a favourite flavouring for beer for some 2,000 years before the hop took its place. Although the hop was first imported by the Romans, it did not gain universal favour until the fifteenth century. Until then, there had always been a clear distinction between ale and beer as only beer contained hops. Ale was flavoured with a variety of different herbs, the nettle predominating. The nettle flavour is bitter and akin to spinach. It gives a good tang to the malted brew, but lacks the preservative quality of the hop oils.

If you have access to a good crop of nettles it is worthwhile making at least one brew.

450g (1 lb) malt extract   *4 litres (7 pints) water*
175g (6 oz) brown sugar   *Beer yeast*
1kg (2¼ lb) nettle tops

Dissolve the malt and brown sugar in 1.2 litres (2 pints) of warm water. Brown sugar adds a little colour to the beer; so, too, does 15ml (3 teaspoons) of black treacle, although this also adds a subtle additional flavour.

Wash the nettles in cold water to remove any dust and tiny insects. Use only the leaves and upper half of the nettle since the stalk is very tough. Boil the nettle tops in 2.3 litres (4 pints) of water for half an hour and leave them to cool. Strain the liquid onto the malt wort and then top up with cold water. Stir in the yeast, cover and leave to ferment for five or

six days. Remove the frothy scum on the second and fourth days and stir the wort. When the fermentation is finished, stand the beer in a cool place for a couple of days, while some of the sediment settles. Siphon the clearing beer into a clean vessel and stir in 20ml (4 teaspoons) of sugar. When it is completely dissolved, pour the beer into eight 1-pint beer bottles, leaving an air space of 5cm (2 in), and stopper tightly. Leave the beer in a warm room for a few days and then in a cool place for two weeks. Serve it cool. The beer will throw a further deposit in the bottle, so care should be taken when pouring not to disturb the sediment. Try it with crusty bread, Cheddar cheese and spring onions, as our forebears did.

GINGER BEER FOR EVERYONE

One of the delights of young children is ginger-pop, or, at least it was when my own children were young. Maybe coke has superceded it for the young children of today. But many people still enjoy a glass of cold ginger beer by itself or blended with some home-brewed ale to make a ginger beer shandy.

Ginger beer is easy to make and ready for drinking in a few days. It can be made in different versions: for children, almost non-alcoholic, or for adults. The only point to watch is the amount of sugar you use as bottling the beer with far too much sugar still fermenting causes the bottle to explode. The two recipes that follow will not blow up.

Recipe A
The first recipe makes eight 1-pint bottles of ginger pop for children.

60g (2 oz) root ginger   *5ml (1 teaspoon)*
2 fresh lemons   *granulated dried yeast*
125g (4½ oz) sugar   *5 litres (1 gallon) water*
15g (½ oz) cream of tartar   *Saccharin tablets*

Bruise the hard, dry, ginger roots with a steak hammer or rolling pin, thinly peel the lemons and place both ingredients in a polythene bin, together with the sugar and cream of tartar. Pour on 1.2 litres (2 pints) of boiling water, stir until the sugar is dissolved, then cover and leave to cool. The hot water also helps extract the flavours from the lemons and the ginger. Squeeze the juice from the lemons. Add the lemon juice, top up to the 5-litre (1-gallon) level with cold water and finally add the yeast granules to the polythene bin. Stir again, cover the bin and leave it in a warm place for 24 hours – no more. Remove any scum or froth and slowly strain the beer into clean screw-stoppered bottles that have previously been used for beer or other fizzy drinks. Screw-stoppered spirit, sherry, vermouth or other wine bottle are not strong enough and should not be used. Add two or three saccharin tablets to each bottle and seal them securely. Leave the beer in a cool place for another 24 hours and it is then ready for drinking. This ginger beer contains only 1% alcohol and may safely be given to children.

Recipe B
The more usual recipe calls for 450g (1 lb) sugar instead of 125g (4½ oz).

60g (2 oz) root ginger	*5ml (1 teaspoon)*
2 fresh lemons	*granulated dried yeast*
450g (1 lb) sugar	*5 litres (1 gallon) water*
15g (½ oz) cream of tartar	

Bruise the hard, dry, ginger roots with a steak hammer or rolling pin, thinly peel the lemons and place both ingredients in a polythene bin, together with the sugar and cream of tartar. Pour on 1.2 litres (2 pints) of boiling water, stir until the sugar is dissolved, then cover and leave to cool. Squeeze the juice from the lemons. Add the lemon juice and the yeast granules to the polythene bin and top up with cold water to the 5-litre (1-gallon) mark. Stir again, cover the bin and leave to ferment in a warm place for seven days until it is virtually finished. Bottle it, adding saccharin tablets if desired, together with 2.5ml (½ teaspoon) of sugar per pint bottle. Stopper the bottles tightly and leave them in a warm place for two or three days, then keep them in a cool store. Serve this beer nice and cold, too, but remember that it contains about 5% alcohol, as much as a good beer and nearly half as much as many table wines. A glass of this ginger beer has a satisfaction about it and makes a splendid half of a ginger beer shandy. The only other needs are a warm day and a good thirst.

The Footpath by Myles Birket Foster

July

There is a tendency among lazy amateur winemakers to sprinkle a dried yeast on a must and leave it to get on by itself. Usually, fermentation will eventually start and eventually finish, but now and then you can strike a dud yeast and fermentation won't start at all or else is very slow and may even pack up for no apparent reason.

The winemaker seeking to achieve the best quality possible always activates the yeast first. Recent research in California and Australia recommends the preparation of a starter equal to 5% of the must to be fermented. In 5 litres (1 gallon) that is 225ml (8 fl oz), in a 23-litre (5-gallon) batch you should use at least 1.2 litres (2 pints) of starter.

Dried yeasts, the scientists report, are best rehydrated in plain water at the relatively high temperature of 38°–43°C (100°–110°F). It is interesting to note that our forebears always activated bakers' yeast in tepid water or at 'blood heat'. The reason for this is now understood, but the explanation is technical and not necessary here. Although plain water is recommended, a well-diluted grape juice also has merit since the start of fermentation can actually be seen with the consequent assurance that the yeast is alive, well and working. Sometimes only a few hours are needed for the yeast to become active.

At this stage best results are obtained by fermenting white musts at an even temperature between 13° and 18°C (55° and 64°F), and red musts at 20°–24°C (68°–75°F). More alcohol is produced and the flavour is enhanced.

Reaping Corn: Labours of the Month, July, from the late 15c. French Playfair Book of Hours

the pectic enzyme is essential. When the must is cool, add as much as is recommended by the manufacturer of the brand you have. It helps to extract the juice and other constituents and ensures a haze-free wine. Also add 1 crushed Campden tablet, replace the cover and leave the bin of fruit and water in a warm place such as the airing cupboard for 24 hours.

Next day, add an active yeast with nutrient and ferment on the pulp for three days, keeping the fruit cap submerged with a large plate or something similar that will not be affected by the acid. Do not use metal. Strain out and press the fruit dry, stir in the sugar, pour the must into a fermentation jar, top up, fit an airlock and ferment to dryness.

As the wine begins to clear, rack the new wine into a clean jar, add 1 Campden tablet, top up, bung tight, label and store for nine months. Siphon the wine into bottles each containing one crushed saccharin tablet. Experience shows that this wine is the more enjoyable if the edge has been taken off the dryness.

Store the bottles for a further three months and then serve the wine cold with roast lamb, new peas and new potatoes. Summer wine with summer food, it makes life worth living.

SUMMER WINE

In Australia 'Summer Wine' is the name that Kaiser Stuhl – one of the largest wine co-operatives in the world – has given to a sparkling white wine. I find it quite delicious although a shade sweet. My summer wine is made from the soft fruits of summer. I first made it in July 1947 when I lived in Kent. I think I have made it every year since then, usually from fruits that I have grown myself.

The secret of this wine is to use as many different fruits as you can and not too many of any single one : black, red and white currants, although not too many black, gooseberries, raspberries and strawberries, a few early blackberries perhaps, some cherries, especially a few morellos if you can get them, a few golden plums and some of those little seedless grapes now in the shops. You need about 1.8kg (4 lb) but the precise figure is not critical, indeed, I often add a few more of the grapes, usually 500g (18 oz).

1.8kg (4 lb) mixed	4 litres (7 pints) boiling
summer fruit	water
1kg (2¼ lb) sugar	Bordeaux yeast and
Pectic enzyme	nutrient
2 Campden tablets	Saccharin tablets

Stalk, stone and wash the fruit, mash it with a potato masher on your hands and fingers, then pour the boiling water over it. Cover and leave it to cool. The fruit contains enough acid even when diluted, but

WHEAT WINE

A good, strong, full-bodied wine can be made with wheat as a major ingredient. The starch is not readily fermentable by the normal wine yeast, but by using *saccharomyces diastaticus* – known as cereal yeast – some starch can be converted into alcohol. Gluten will be extracted and this gives the wine a full body and the grain flavour also comes over into the wine. It needs to be matured for some two or three years or more to reach its peak, but by then it is very smooth and makes an unusual, but acceptable dessert wine.

675g (1½ lb) wheat	1 each lemon, orange and
500g (18 oz) raisins	grapefruit
250g (9 oz) concentrated	4 litres (7 pints) water
white grape juice	Cereal yeast and nutrient
1kg (2¼ lb) sugar	1 Campden tablet

Wash the grains in cold water to remove the dust and soak them in enough hot water to cover them for 1 hour to soften them. Shake off the loose moisture, lay the grains on a formica surface and crush them with a rolling pin. If it is more convenient, you may coarsely grind them in a mincer or food processor.

Wash and finely chop the raisins; thinly pare the fruits and place the parings with the chopped dried fruit into a bin with the crushed wheat. Pour 3.4 litres (6 pints) boiling water over these ingredients, cover the bin and leave to cool.

Meanwhile, cut the citrus fruits in half and squeeze

out the juice. Strain the juice and then add it to the cool must, together with the concentrated grape juice and the pre-activated yeast. Place a china plate over the fruit to keep it submerged, then cover the bin. Leave it in a warm place for one week.

Strain out, press the mash dry and discard it; dissolve the sugar in 575ml (1 pint) of hot water and when cool, add half of it to the fermenting must. Pour this into a fermentation jar, fit an airlock and leave it alone for one week. Pour the remaining syrup into a sterilised bottle, cork it and keep it cool. Slowly stir in half this syrup after the first week and the remainder the following week.

When fermentation has finished, move the jar to a cool place and as soon as the wine begins to clear, siphon it into a sterilised storage jar. Top up, add 1 Campden tablet, bung tight, label and store the jar in a cool place for eight to ten weeks, then rack again. By this time the wine should be bright and ready to put into final storage for from twelve to eighteen months.

In the unlikely event of the wine still being hazy, pour a little wine into a saucer and add a few drops of ordinary yellow tincture of iodine. If the wine darkens, turning blue, brown or black, then the presence of starch is indicated. Some fungal amylase – a starch-reducing enzyme – must be added in accordance with the manufacturer's instructions on the packet. Amylase can be purchased from home-brew shops.

If the colour of the hazy wine doesn't change, then ordinary proprietary finings should be added to clear the wine. These finings normally clear a wine within a week or ten days, after which the wine must be racked again. Add 1 crushed Campden tablet and store in the cool.

Keep the wine for a further six to nine months after bottling and finally serve it cool with shortbread or sweet cake. If you enjoy a strong, sweet, full-bodied wine, then this wheat wine is well worth making and keeping long enough to mature completely.

GOOSEBERRY 'BUBBLY'

Of all the fruits used to make wine, I think that the gooseberry is perhaps the best. It can be used to make superb still wines strongly reminiscent of Hock as well as outstanding sparkling wines.

One year I made wine from each of three different varieties of gooseberry and subsequently compared them. The wine made from a variety called 'Careless' was best, with 'Leveller' in second place. Dessert gooseberry varieties are not usually as successful as the culinary varieties.

Another special advantage of the gooseberry is that it freezes perfectly and can be kept until it is convenient for you to make it into wine. I have often made gooseberry wine in December, because I was too busy in July.

Always wash the fruit before use and I top and tail mine, although I know that some winemakers feel that this is not necessary. Because the berries are hard, pour hot water over them and leave them to cool. They are then soft enough to be crushed with the hands. Each berry has to be broken so that the goodness can be extracted. Because the gooseberry flavour is quite strong, I use only 1.5kg (3 lb) to the 5 litres (1 gallon) and include a couple of ripe bananas to increase the body for still wines. Always include some grape, either as fresh grapes, sultanas or concentrated white grape juice.

1.5kg (3 lb) green gooseberries	4 litres (7 pints) hot water
250g (9 oz) concentrated white grape juice	Pectic enzyme
5ml (1 teaspoon) citric acid	2 Campden tablets
2.5ml ($\frac{1}{2}$ teaspoon) grape tannin	2 sachets Champagne yeast and nutrient
800g (1$\frac{3}{4}$ lb) sugar	70g (2$\frac{1}{2}$ oz) caster sugar
	Saccharin tablets

Pour the hot water over the gooseberries and when cool, mash them and stir in the pectic enzyme, acid, tannin and 1 crushed Campden tablet. Cover and leave for 24 hours. Add the concentrated grape juice, one sachet of activated Champagne yeast and nutrient and ferment on the pulp for three days, timing from when the fruit is seen floating on the surface. Then keep the fruit submerged with a china plate.

Strain out and press the fruit dry, stir in the sugar, pour the must into a fermentation jar, fit an airlock and ferment out in a cool place. Rack the wine into a storage jar, add 1 Campden tablet, top up, bung tight and store in a cold place. As soon as the wine is bright, rack again.

When the wine is six months old, stir in 70g (2 oz) caster sugar and another Champagne yeast and nutrient. Fit an airlock, place the jar in a warm position and as soon as fermentation starts pour the wine into six sterilised Champagne bottles. Fit softened, hollow-domed, plastic stoppers and wire cages to keep them on. Lay the bottles on their sides in a warm room for two weeks and then on their sides in a cool store for at least six months.

Stand the bottles upside down in a wine carton for several weeks, giving them a daily shake and twist to encourage the sediment to settle into the hollow-domed stoppers. When this has been achieved, freeze the stopper in crushed ice and salt, remove the cage and stopper containing the sediment in the frozen wine, sweeten with a crushed saccharin tablet or two, fit a clean, soft stopper and replace the cage. This splendid wine should be served cold.

cheaper. The cartons usually contain 5.4kg (12 lb) of fruit packed on the farm and therefore, still pretty fresh. The 'Leveller' variety is suitable for this recipe.

5.4kg (12 lb) green gooseberries	Campden tablets
1kg (2¼ lb) concentrated Hock-type grape juice	5ml (1 teaspoon) grape tannin
8 ripe bananas	13.5 litres (3 gallons) water
3kg (6½ lb) sugar	Hock wine yeast and nutrient
30g (1 oz) citric acid	
30g (1 oz) pectic enzyme	Saccharin tablets

Wash, top, tail and crush the gooseberries, peel and thinly slice or mash the bananas. Pour the water into a bin, add the acid, tannin, pectic enzyme and 4 crushed Campden tablets. When they have dissolved, add the gooseberries and bananas. Cover the bin and leave it in a warm place for 24 hours while the enzyme dissolves the pectin. Next day, stir in the concentrated grape juice and the activated wine yeast. Ferment on the pulp for four days, pressing down the floating fruit cap twice daily.

Strain out, press dry and discard the fruit. Stir in the sugar, making sure that it is completely dissolved. Pour the must into a large jar or into four standard demijohns. If necessary, top up with cold water, fit airlocks and ferment out to dryness in a cool place (15°C/60°F).

Move the jars to a cold floor for a few days to encourage the sediment to settle, then siphon the clearing wine into clean jars and add 1 Campden tablet per 5 litres (1 gallon). Cork, label and store until the wine is bright, then rack again. Keep the wine for nine months, then bottle it and keep it for another three or four months. Sweeten each bottle slightly with 1 saccharin tablet per bottle. Serve the wine well chilled with poultry, pork or fish.

GOOSEBERRY HOCK

No apology is needed for writing about the gooseberry again, since it is such a splendid fruit for making into white wine of many types. Some 200 years or so ago, it was made commercially and used to 'improve' imported white wines that were tired and weak from the constant jolting that they received on their journey by land and sea from France and Germany to the United Kingdom. When revivified with gooseberry wine, the imported white wines were then sold at a higher price.

This process works equally well in reverse and is the main reason for adding concentrated grape juice to fruit wines. It gives the wines some vinosity. One can of concentrate is sufficient for 18 litres (4 gallons) of fruit wine. This recipe makes twenty-four bottles of gooseberry 'hock', which works out at less than half a bottle a week for one year. If you agree that this is too little, then double or treble the quantities. Be sure that all your equipment is sterilised with a sulphite solution, never omit the Campden tablets recommended in the recipe and then nothing can go wrong. Cleanliness is next to godliness!

A whole carton or box of gooseberries can often be obtained from your greengrocer 1 or 2p per pound

BLACKCURRANT WINE

Blackcurrants have such a strong flavour and high acidity that they do not make a good table wine. They can be made into a dessert wine that needs very long keeping but their greatest use, in my opinion, is in blending. I always include a few in my 'Summer Fruit' wine, both for colour and flavour. I also freeze some and save them for my Autumn Red wine where their acidity, colour and flavour are of great value. There is, too, another recipe that I like to make up in the summer when blackcurrants are fresh and full of vitamins. Blackcurrant Rum is in the same family of liqueurs as Sloe Gin and is very well worth making for those cold winter nights. When returning from a holiday abroad, I always bring home my full allowance of spirits in the form of vodka, gin and white

by an old market gardener. Morello cherries are, or perhaps I should say were, very plentiful in Kent especially around Sittingbourne. In the days when this recipe was evolved, money was scarcer than it is today, life was simple, pleasures were often home-made and morello cherry ale was one of them. My elderly friend described it as 'the poor man's cherry brandy'. I have made and enjoyed it many times.

The morello cherries should be black ripe but these are difficult to obtain since the birds are less fussy than us and will eat them whilst still a bright red. However, one can sometimes see them at the green-grocers, in home freezer centres or in bottles at supermarkets. Make sure you get morello cherries and not just black cherries because the flavour is different. I like the fresh morellos myself and now is the time for them. A suitable container for fermentation is a large sweet jar. The size is right and the neck is not too small. It is important to use a Tokay yeast to ensure a successful fermentation to a high alcohol content. Other yeast may give up too soon.

900g (2 lb) fresh, frozen   *675g (1½ lb) demerara*
   or bottled morello   *sugar – not too dark*
   cherries   *Tokay yeast and nutrient*
2.3 litres (4 pints) strong
   home-brewed ale

rum, for I know that I shall want them for my liqueurs. White rum is important for this recipe since it is colourless and free from caramel.

225g (8 oz) caster sugar   *75cl (26⅔ fl oz) white*
225g (8 oz) fresh   *rum*
   blackcurrants

Sterilise a 1-litre bottle and pour the caster sugar into it through a dry funnel. Select the largest and choicest blackcurrants, remove the stalks, wash the berries, mash them and poke them through the funnel into the bottle. Pour in the rum, and then cork and label the bottle. Shake the bottle gently each day for one week until the sugar is completely dissolved and the colour well extracted from the blackcurrants. Strain out the blackcurrants, pressing them firmly until they are dry. Do not discard them but mix them into some apple pulp to make a blackcurrant and apple pie that's different! Pour the blackcurrant rum into assorted bottles, seal and label them, store them in a cool place and keep them until Christmas.

Remove the stalks from the cherries, wash them and prick them all over with a needle. Place them in the washed and sterilised jar, sprinkle on half the sugar and slowly pour the beer down the side of the jar so as not to create a foaming head. Stir the fruit and sugar and beer gently until the sugar is dissolved, then add the activated yeast and nutrient.

Cover the jar with a polythene bag secured with a rubber band and leave the jar in a warm place. Ten days later add half the remaining sugar and one week later still, stir in the rest. Leave the jar in the warmth until fermentation is finished and then in a cool place for another two weeks. Strain out the cherries and serve them in an open flan topped with cream! When the sediment has settled, siphon the clear beverage into six half-size wine bottles, cork, label and keep for a few months. Made now this drink should be ready by Christmas but treat it with respect.

 ## MORELLO CHERRY ALE

Although we now think of ale or beer as being exclusively flavoured with hops, it was not always so. Indeed hops have only been exclusively used during the past 300 years or so. Previously many people preferred the taste of nettles or yarrow or other herbs, and fruit ales were very popular.

This recipe comes from Kent and was given to me

August

The recipes indicate a quantity of water to be used but this can often be no more than an approximate quantity. The two main variables are the juiciness of the fruit you use and the determination with which you press it. If you have more than enough to fill your demijohn, ferment the surplus in a suitably sized bottle plugged with cotton wool and stand it beside the jar. At the racking stages, this can be used for topping up. Collect small surplus quantities of different wines and store them in a single bottle to top up any wine you are making. Keep the red and white separate, of course.

Similarly, if you have a quantity of wine left in a jar after racking, pour this into a bottle, stopper it and stand it in the refrigerator. When it clears, siphon off the wine and discard the sediment. Keep this wine for topping up. With a little care, no wine need be wasted.

A further use for these wines collected from the bottoms of different jars, blended together, cleared and racked, is in cooking. Stew fruit in this wine instead of water, marinade fish or meat in it, or pour it over roasts. Indeed, whenever a recipe calls for wine, use this wine. As long as the wine smells clean and wholesome it is good to use.

The Market Cart by W. F. Witherington

2kg (4½ lb) fresh pea pods
250g (9 oz) concentrated
  white grape juice
900g (2 lb) sugar
4 litres (7 pints) water
15ml (3 teaspoons) citric
  acid

2.5ml (½ teaspoon) grape
  tannin
1 Campden tablet
Hock or Chablis yeast
  and nutrient

Cut up the pea pods and boil them gently in the water for about 20 minutes until they are cooked. Leave them to cool, then strain the liquid into a fermentation bin. Stir in the concentrated grape juice, the sugar, citric acid, tannin, nutrient and an active yeast. When all is dissolved, pour the must into a fermentation jar, top it up if necessary with cold water, fit an airlock and leave the jar in a cool place until fermentation is finished.

Move the jar into a cooler place to encourage the sediment to settle, then rack the wine into a clean jar, add 1 Campden tablet, bung tight, label and store for three or four months until the wine is bright. Siphon the wine into six clean bottles, cork, label and keep for a further two or three months before serving the wine nicely chilled with poached, baked or grilled fish. It is surprisingly enjoyable.

BROAD BEAN WINE

We know that country folk throughout the nineteenth century made wine from some very unusual ingredients, including mangel-wurzels. I know, too, that many winemakers tell me that they are making wine from this or that 'just as an experiment'. The recipes given in these articles are never experimental. They have all been made many times and produce sound and drinkable wines when properly served with appropriate food. Palates vary considerably, however, and a fine dry table wine does not please those people who like a Sauternes-style wine with everything. You will be quite surprised that such an unlikely ingredient as broad beans produces such a splendid wine. If you have a surplus of beans this year, do make this wine. Remember to wait until the husks of the beans are too old for culinary use by when the flavour is strongest. You need a fair number of shelled beans, around 2kg (4½ lb).

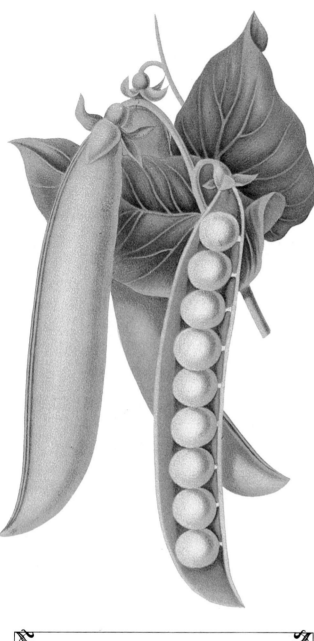

PEA POD WINE

The keen winemaker sees a source of wine in everything from the garden whether it be fruit, flowers, herbs or vegetables. Shucked and unwanted pea pods are no exception. To be used for making wine, however, they should be green, fresh and tender. Mouldy, wet or dried-out pods are useless. The better the pod the better the wine.

About 2kg (4½ lb) of empty pods are needed to make 5 litres (1 gallon) of a light dry table wine. It has a green tint in its hue and the bouquet is 'fresh' and pleasant. You will find it surprisingly enjoyable when served cold with a fish or cold meat salad. As always include some concentrated grape juice of the Hock or Chablis type to give body and vinosity to the wine and use a matching yeast. Vegetables have little or no acid so a fair bit must be added.

2kg (4½ lb) old broad
  beans
250g (9 oz) concentrated
  white grape juice
800g (1¾ lb) sugar

10g (2 teaspoons) citric
  acid
4 litres (7 pints) water
1 Campden tablet
Hock yeast and nutrient

Like all other vegetables used for making wine, the beans must be boiled gently to extract the flavour and nutrients. Perhaps 'slowly simmered until they are tender' is a better phrase because one must be careful not to allow the skins to break or the wine will become difficult to clear. Use the bean water for the wine and eat the beans with a mushroom or parsley sauce. If you can't eat them all at once, the surplus can be frozen until required. After cooking the broad beans, strain the liquid into a bin and stir in the sugar and citric acid. Cover the bin and leave it to cool.

Stir in the concentrated grape juice and an active yeast with nutrient, then pour the must into a fermentation jar, fit an airlock and ferment out. Rack into a clean jar, add 1 Campden tablet to prevent infection and oxidation, top up, bung tight, label and store for six months. Bottle and keep the wine for a few months longer.

Serve the wine nicely chilled with boiled bacon and cabbage or similar dishes.

PEACH PARFAIT

Peaches and other stone fruit are plentiful at this time of the year. A complete trayful of peaches bought at a wholesale market may be a worthwhile buy. A friendly greengrocer might even let you have some that are a little over-ripe and cheaper.

Some winemakers use peaches 'as they come', but

in my view it is better to peel them, cut away any bad portions and remove the stones. If the stone is left in, it imparts a taste like nail polish to the finished wine that I find unpleasant. Nectarines are even more expensive than peaches, but if ever sufficient come your way at a reasonable price, then they, too, can be made into a wine of a similar style, albeit with a different flavour.

2kg (4¼ lb) fresh peach pulp
1kg (2¼ lb) seedless grapes
750g (1½ lb) sugar
15ml (3 teaspoons) citric acid
5ml (1 teaspoon) pectic enzyme

2 Campden tablets
2.8 litres (5 pints) water
15ml (3 teaspoons) glycerine
Sauternes yeast and nutrient
100g (3½ oz) lactose

Weigh the prepared good fruit, crush it and place it in a bin. Pick over the grapes, wash them in a sulphite solution and crush them. Pour the water, citric acid, pectic enzyme and 1 crushed Campden tablet into the bin, and then add the crushed grapes. Cover and leave for 24 hours. Next day, stir in an activated yeast and ferment on the pulp for five days, pressing down the fruit cap twice daily.

Strain out the pulp and press it gently, stir in the sugar, pour the must into a fermentation jar, top up with cold water if necessary, fit an airlock, label and leave the wine to ferment out.

When fermentation is finished, rack the wine into a clean jar, stir in the glycerine and lactose. Add 1 Campden tablet to protect the wine from infection, top up, bung tight and store in a cool, dark place until the wine is bright. Rack again.

Bottle this wine in half-size bottles and keep it until it is ten to twelve months old. It is a rich tasting, full-bodied, slightly sweet wine that may be sweetened still further with caster sugar or saccharin if you so wish, at the time of serving. The result will be a sweet dessert wine, similar in style to the ever-popular Sauternes. Serve it nicely chilled with sweet food.

FRESH APRICOT WINE

In summertime fresh apricots can be bought at the greengrocers. They are not only splendid when stewed in wine and served as a dessert, but also when made into wine. They make a light dry table wine that accompanies *sole bonne femme* and similar dishes to perfection. I enjoy it, too, as an accompaniment to smoked haddock poached with mushrooms in milk and served with a sauce made from the liquid. The crispness of this wine makes a marvellous match for the fishy sauce. Greengages may be used instead of

The following recipe will help you make a daily glass (or two) of a sherry-type wine. The ingredients are for eighteen bottles, but increase the quantities *pro rata* to make more.

5.4kg (12 lb) ripe Victoria plums	*15ml (3 teaspoons) pectic enzyme*
450g (1 lb) dried apricot pieces	*3 Campden tablets*
1kg (2¼ lb) dry sherry-style concentrated grape juice	*5ml (1 teaspoon) grape tannin*
3.6kg (8 lb) sugar	*10ml (2 teaspoons) yeast nutrient*
30g (1 oz) tartaric acid	*2 3mg vitamin B tablets*
60g (2 oz) gypsum	*11.25 litres (2½ gallons) water*
15g (½ oz) cream of tartar	*Sherry Flor yeast*

Wash, chop and soak the dried apricot pieces overnight in 1.2 litres (2 pints) of hot water. Pour 9 litres (2 gallons) of cold water into a polythene bin. Add the tartaric acid, pectic enzyme, tannin, gypsum, cream of tartar and 3 Campden tablets. When these have dissolved, add the juice and pulp of the apricots.

Wash, stone and crush the Victoria plums and add them to the bin. Cover and leave it in a warm place for 24 hours. Stir in the concentrated grape juice, nutrient, vitamin B tablets and an activated sherry yeast. Ferment on the pulp for four days, pressing down the fruit cap twice daily.

Strain out the pulp through a nylon bag, press dry and discard. Stir in 1kg (2¼ lb) sugar and continue fermentation in the bin. Keep the bin covered with a lid or sheet of polythene secured with a rubber band. One week later, stir in another 1kg (2¼ lb) sugar and top the bin up to the 13.5-litre (3-gallon) mark with cold water.

After another week stir in the third 1kg (2¼ lb) sugar and after one more week the rest of the sugar. (If you have a hydrometer, check the must regularly and add the sugar each time the reading falls to 1.004. If the fermentation slows down, add the last of the sugar in smaller quantities as needed. In this way the maximum quantity of alcohol will be formed – perhaps as much as 17%.)

Finish the wine dry or nearly so, then move it to a cool place while the sediment settles. After a few days rack it into storage jars, leaving an air space in each jar to help in the formation of that special sherry flavour. Plug the necks of the jars with cotton wool. Do not use cork or rubber bungs. Label and store the wine until it is bright.

Rack the wine into clean jars and add one bottle of dry sherry shared between the jars. Replace the cotton wool plugs and store for about two years. Bottle and serve it nicely chilled.

apricots, but do remember to remove the stones or they will impart an unpleasant flavour.

2kg (4½ lb) fresh apricots	*4 litres (7 pints) water*
250g (9 oz) concentrated white grape juice	*Pectic enzyme*
10ml (2 teaspoons) citric acid	*1 Campden tablet*
800g (1¾ lb) sugar	*Chablis or Burgundy yeast and nutrient*

Gently heat the apricots and one glass of white wine together in a saucepan and remove the stones as the fruit softens. Add them to 3.4 litres (6 pints) of cold water containing 5ml (1 teaspoon) of pectic enzyme and the citric acid. Cover and leave for 24 hours.

Next day add the concentrated grape juice, the activated yeast and nutrient. Ferment on the pulp for four days keeping the fruit submerged and the bin covered. Strain out the pulp, stir in the sugar, pour the must into a fermentation jar, top up, fit an airlock and ferment out. Rack into a clean jar, top up, add 1 Campden tablet, bung tight and store in a cold dark place until the wine is bright. Rack again, store for three months, then bottle and keep for a further three months. No additional sweetening should be added. The wine should be served quite dry and nicely chilled. I have especially enjoyed it with poached smoked haddock.

SWEET WHITE WINE

No true winemaker can walk past a greengrocer's shop these days without getting ideas that set the taste buds tingling. The gorgeous array usually includes pineapples, melons, plums, peaches, apricots, bananas, apples, oranges and the choice of black and white grapes. Some fruits seem outrageously expensive and others remarkably cheap.

My eyes always light upon the small, seedless grapes from Cyprus that are now in full abundance. Not so many years ago, I used to buy a whole tray of perfect grapes for £1, but they cost so much more now that I no longer think that they are worth buying for wine. You need around 8kg (18 lb) of grapes to make 5 litres (1 gallon) of wine and unless you have a very cheap source of supply, Cypriot grape wine may cost you as much as a bottle of commercial wine. If you can get some good, loose grapes cheaply, they are worth having, if only to mix in with some other fruits. Italian wine grapes will soon be available from importers who cater for the home winemaking market. They are worth waiting for.

Peaches seem a better buy at present, especially if you can get some of the very ripe ones a little cheaper. You need about 2kg (4½ lb) of them since there is bound to be a little waste. You will also need a couple of very ripe bananas and a large fresh lemon. The bananas add some extra flavour and body, while the lemon sharpens the taste. The citric acid in addition to the lemon is an important ingredient in this wine and should not be omitted. The flavour, body, sweetness and 12% alcohol, need to be balanced with the additional acid or it will taste medicinal.

2kg (4½ lb) peaches	*4 litres (7 pints) water*
2 ripe bananas	*Pectic enzyme*
225g (½ lb) sultanas	*2 Campden tablets*
1 large lemon	*15ml (3 teaspoons)*
20g (¾ oz) citric acid	*glycerine*
2.5ml (½ teaspoon) grape	*Sauternes yeast and*
tannin	*nutrient*
800g (1¾ lb) white sugar	

Cut away any damaged part of the peaches, remove the stones and, if you can, peel the peaches. Mash them and the peeled bananas and chop up the sultanas. Thinly pare the lemon and squeeze out the juice, discarding the pith and pips. Place all the fruit, the lemon parings and juice in a mashing bin. Add the citric acid, tannin, pectic enzyme and 1 crushed Campden tablet. Pour on the cold water, stir, cover and leave in a warm place for 24 hours.

Next day, add an actively fermenting yeast, replace the cover and ferment on the pulp for four days. Keep the fruit submerged with a plate for the whole of this period. Strain out the pulp through a fine nylon sieve or a bag but do not press it. Stir in the sugar, pour the must into a fermentation jar, fit an airlock and ferment out.

Move the jar to a cool place for two or three days to encourage the solid particles to settle, then siphon the wine into a clean jar. Add the glycerine, 1 Campden tablet, top up, bung tight, label and leave the jar in a cold place until the wine is bright.

Siphon the clear wine into bottles and sweeten each one to taste with saccharin. Two crushed tablets per bottle is usually enough. Cork, label and keep for six months in a cool place.

Serve this full-flavoured, full-bodied, sweet white wine well chilled with the dessert course of a meal or with sweet biscuits.

CYSER

Apples and honey have long been recognised as sources of nourishment especially suitable for the human body. Cyser is the ancient name of a mead containing apple juice as well as honey. It is not made as often today as it deserves to be, although it is now easier to make than ever before and is quite inexpensive in relation to its beneficial quality.

2 litres (3½ pints)	*5ml (1 teaspoon) citric*
unsweetened apple	*acid*
juice	*2 litres (3½ pints) water*
450g (1 lb) pale blended	*All-purpose yeast and*
honey	*wine nutrient*
350g (12 oz) demerara	*1 Campden tablet*
sugar	

Activate the yeast in the usual way. Boil the sugar and citric acid in 575ml (1 pint) of water for 20 minutes and leave it to cool. Dissolve the honey in 575ml (1 pint) of hot water and leave it to cool.

Pour the apple juice, diluted honey and sugar syrup into a fermentation jar, top up with cold water, stir in the yeast, fit an airlock, tie on a contents label and leave the jar in a warm position while fermentation is progressing.

When fermentation ends, move the jar to a cool place to encourage the sediment to settle. Siphon the clearing cyser into a clean jar, add 1 Campden tablet to prevent oxidation and infection, top up with cold boiled water, fit a good bung or cork and store for three months while the cyser matures. It may then be bottled and improves if kept for a few months longer.

Cyser is a light dry wine in which both the flavour of the honey and the apple are discernible, but not pronounced. Some people prefer this wine to be not quite dry and so it may be sweetened just before serving it, with either a little honey or sugar.

It should, of course, be served cold and makes a

long keeping. It will need some two years in bulk storage before being bottled in half pints, appropriately labelled and stored in a cool place for a further year. Indeed, it will keep for five years and longer in excellent condition. As a souvenir of the Jubilee it will bring joy and pleasure on the sixteen occasions a bottle is opened.

900g (2 lb) pale malt flour	100g ($3\frac{1}{2}$ oz) crystal malt grains
225g ($\frac{1}{2}$ lb) Super Flavex malt syrup	Brown sugar
9 litres (2 gallons) water	30g (1 oz) Fuggles hops
225g ($\frac{1}{2}$ lb) pale malt grains	15g ($\frac{1}{2}$ oz) Bullion hops
	Madeira 'Super' wine yeast

Dissolve the malt flour and malt syrup in warm water and pour it into a preserving pan or stock pot. The pan used should be made from stainless steel, heavy-duty aluminium or unchipped enamel. Add the malt grains and the Fuggles hops, wetting them thoroughly with the liquid. Bring the wort to a gently rolling boil and continue this for 45 minutes. Add the Bullion hops – don't forget to wet them – and continue the boil for a further 15 minutes. If possible, keep the pan covered to minimise evaporation. Remove the pan from the heat, strain out the hops and grains and wash them with some hot water to remove the last traces of malt sugar and flavour. Add the washings to the wort, cover and cool as quickly as possible, then check the specific gravity with a hydrometer. Stir in sufficient water and brown sugar to increase the quantity to 4.8 litres ($8\frac{1}{2}$ pints) and the specific gravity to 1.100.

Six hours before brewing the beer, prepare a starter bottle from a sachet of Madeira 'Super' wine yeast and make sure that it is fermenting vigorously before pitching it into the cool wort. Check the temperature before doing so and reduce it to 20°C (68° F).

Give the wort a good stir and leave it in a covered bin for a couple of days before pouring it carefully into a fermentation jar and fitting an airlock. Maintain a cool temperature and be patient with the fermentation. It may well take as long as six weeks before the ale becomes still and begins to clear. Siphon it off the sediment into a sterilised jar, top up with cold water, seal, label and store until the ale is bright, then rack into sixteen half-pint bottles and store for two years.

It is most important to get a perfect seal when you bottle the ale. A cylindrical cork may be pushed just below the level of the bottle mouth and then covered with sealing wax. The hardest part is waiting for this beer to mature. However, it is not one that is made every week, nor one to be quaffed lightly or quickly. Treat the high alcohol content of this beer with great respect.

good companion to picnic meals in the summer. Not being too strong it is a good luncheon beverage. It will not keep for many years, however, and is best drunk whilst it is still young, say, one year.

Pineapple, orange or grapefruit juice make acceptable alternatives to the apple juice, but you need to double the quantity of sugar used. The result is always a very suitable lunch-time apéritif, palate-cleansing and appetising without the subsequent soporific effects of sherry. Such a beverage should not be called a cyser, however, but rather a melomel – a mixture of honey and fruit juice other than apple or grape. When grape juice is added, the mead is called pyment. The bottled grape juice available in supermarkets is quite suitable. They all do you good!

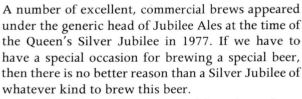

JUBILEE ALE

A number of excellent, commercial brews appeared under the generic head of Jubilee Ales at the time of the Queen's Silver Jubilee in 1977. If we have to have a special occasion for brewing a special beer, then there is no better reason than a Silver Jubilee of whatever kind to brew this beer.

The following recipe suggested by a home-brew champion, is fairly easy to brew, but alas, does need

September

Once upon a time September was the busiest month of the year for winemaking. Blackberries, elderberries, sloes, damsons, apples, pears, quinces and plums, all cried out for attention at the same time. Often there would also be imported grapes in the shops. For a lucky few there might be mulberries, loganberries, even bilberries available. I found that letting it be known that I was a winemaker often brought a knock on the door from a friend with a box of fruit surplus to his needs. A bottle of the resultant wine was a very cheap price to pay.

September still is a very busy month although the pressure can be diminished by cleaning and freezing some of the fruit until a more convenient time. It is well worthwhile making the maximum quantity of wine that your facilities will permit. Sometimes these can be temporarily extended by makeshift methods. For example, a large polythene bag in a strong cardboard carton can be used as a fermentation vessel. Gather the neck together with a rubber band. You may be able to fit an airlock into it. If not, fold it over, the pressure of the gas coming off will prevent air from entering. Be on the safe side and put one bag inside another – just in case! The double thickness is a safety factor. Use food-grade polythene of course. Nevertheless, keep an eye on the box for leaks but I have always been successful – so far. I've often used this method for fermenting up to 45kg (100 lb) of apples.

The 23-litre (5-gallon) polythene-lined sherry cartons are very useful for fermenting and for short-term storage. The cap and tap unscrew and can be replaced with a bored bung and airlock, or the tap can be turned to open and plugged with cotton wool.

Make sure that you have a good supply of sulphite, Campden tablets, citric acid, tannin, yeast nutrient and pure wine yeasts. Acid-indicator pH paper should also be to hand. It is available in rolls off which you tear a strip to dip into the must. When the paper dries, compare its colour with that on the chart supplied. It will at least give you an idea whether the liquid you are testing is low, normal or high in acid – better than not knowing even that much. Acidity is essential for a good bouquet and flavour. The acidity of fruit varies substantially with its ripeness as well as the season in general and the variety in particular.

remove any dust and tiny insects. Activate the yeast by mixing it with 15ml (1 tablespoonful) of concentrated grape juice dissolved in 275ml ($\frac{1}{2}$ pint) of tepid boiled water. Use a standard wine bottle, plug the neck with cotton wool and leave it in a warm place.

Next day wash and crush the blackberries and put in a large pan. Add 2.3 litres (4 pints) of cold water, stir in the tannin, acid, pectic enzyme and 1 crushed Campden tablet. Cover the pan and leave for 24 hours. Add the concentrated grape juice and active yeast to the blackberries and ferment on the pulp for five days stirring gently each day. Strain out the fruit and press it dry. Stir in the sugar, pour the must into a fermentation jar, top up with cold water, fit an air-lock and ferment to dryness.

Rack into a clean jar, top up, bung tight, label and store for two months, then rack again. The wine should now be brilliant and needs a further six months in store before bottling. Keep it for at least another three months and preferably longer. Serve it at room temperature with roast beef.

Picking blackberries by William Bromley

BLACKBERRY TABLE WINE

Cultivated blackberries from the garden will soon be ready for picking and shortly afterwards the hedge-row blackberry. Both varieties make excellent red wine, one for table and the other for dessert wine. They also blend well with other fruits.

Cultivated blackberries are best for making into table wine and so a Burgundy-type concentrated grape juice is needed. Hedgerow blackberries have a stronger flavour, more acid and tannin and therefore make a better dessert wine. They need a Port-type concentrated grape juice. Use a matching yeast for the best results.

2kg (4$\frac{1}{2}$ lb) cultivated blackberries	5ml (1 teaspoon) pectic enzyme
250g (9 oz) Burgundy-type concentrated grape juice	5ml (1 teaspoon) grape tannin
	1 Campden tablet
900g (2 lb) sugar	2.8 litres (5 pints) water
5ml (1 teaspoon) tartaric acid	Burgundy wine yeast and nutrient

Gather the garden blackberries on a dry summer day when they are large and juicy. Avoid half-ripe or damaged berries. Lay them in shallow containers until you are ready to make them into wine, so that you do not squash them prematurely. Remove all the stalks, then rinse the berries under cold water to

BLACKBERRY 'PORT'

This recipe brings back very happy memories for me. Blackberry wine was the first I ever made – back in September 1945. Wild blackberries are needed, so a trip to a country lane or heath is called for. Make the trip on a dry day and preferably a sunny one. Gather the largest and juiciest berries that you can find and, as far as possible, collect them in fairly shallow containers so that they don't get too squashed on the way home. Whilst they are not specifically required, a few fat elderberries or sloes may be included.

2kg (4$\frac{1}{2}$ lb) wild blackberries	5ml (1 teaspoon) grape tannin
450g (1 lb) best raisins	4 litres (7 pints) water
1.25kg (2$\frac{3}{4}$ lb) cane sugar	Pectic enzyme
2 ripe bananas	Campden tablets
10ml (2 teaspoons) citric acid	Port wine yeast and nutrient

As soon as you get the berries home, remove and discard the stalks, then rinse the fruit in cold water to wash away the tiny hairs and any insects. Place the fruit in a mashing bin and crush it with a sterilised potato masher or something similar.

Wash and chop the raisins, preferably buy the big ones with stones but don't break the pips when chopping the raisins as they impart an unpleasant flavour. Add the raisins to the bin. Peel and mash the bananas and add these to the bin.

Meanwhile prepare the port wine yeast starter as described on the sachet so that a very active yeast colony can be added to the must. Ferment on the pulp for the next five days, keeping the pulp submerged with a weighted china plate. Boil the sugar and acid in 575ml (1 pint) of water for 20 minutes and leave it to cool. Pour it into a litre-bottle and stopper it, for it will not all be required at once. Strain out the fruit through a nylon straining bag and press out all the juice you can. Stir in the grape tannin and half the sugar syrup, pour the must into a fermentation jar, leaving space for the rest of the syrup, fit an airlock and place the jar in a steady room temperature of around 21°C (70°F). After five days, add half the remaining syrup and five days later, add the rest of the syrup.

When fermentation is finished, rack the wine into a clean jar, add some wine finings in accordance with the instructions supplied with them and leave the wine in a cool place until the wine is bright. Rack again, taste the wine and, if necessary, sweeten to suit your palate. Label the jar and put it right at the back of your store for at least two years. After bottling, keep the wine a further period of several months. Serve it free from chill after a meal, preferably following an hour in a decanter.

If the wine has been fermented and stored in a brown demijohn, the wine should have a dark red/black robe free from any purplish hue, a clean fruity bouquet and a very smooth texture. The flavour should be complex with only a subtle hint of blackberry. This is a real favourite with many winemakers, in spite of the waiting. If the wine is not kept out of the light it tends to fade to a tawny port colour.

ELDERBERRY, THE GREAT

Sometimes described as the Englishman's grape, the elderberry has long been an ingredient for making wine. It grows all over Europe and used to be added to the grapes from which port wine is made so as to improve and enrich the colour. In France the berries were used in years gone by for the making of a cordial highly regarded as a remedy for winter coughs. In England a similar recipe was used. The berries, after being picked from their stalks, were washed and placed in a large pan that was left on the back of the stove for several days. The juice was then strained off and mixed with honey. Sometimes a few cloves and pieces of ginger were added to the elderberries to enhance the flavour. The result was pleasant enough, if somewhat bitter. Like the grape, elderberries were also dried and added to cakes in place of currants.

By itself the elderberry flavour is too bitter for me and I prefer to mix other fruits in with it. As a result, one can spread one's elderberries over a wide range of wines. The best way to extract the colour and nutritious elements is to heat the elderberries in water (80°C/175°F) for about 20 minutes until they 'dimple'. They contain very little acid and not much sugar but plenty of tannin and flavour. One kilo ($2\frac{1}{4}$ lb) to every 5 litres (1 gallon) is plenty and I often use less. Gather them on a dry day when the berries hang big and black from dark red stalks. Gather them from different trees because there are at least eight varieties of elderberries. When cleaning the berries, discard every scrap of stalk, the bitterness of which is excessive. Rinse them free from dust in cold water and use them at once. If this is not possible, freeze them until it is convenient. I have kept them for as long as two years in excellent condition.

ELDERBERRY TABLE WINE

900g (2 lb) elderberries, cleaned and crushed	5ml (1 teaspoon) pectic enzyme
250g (9 oz) chopped raisins	4 litres (7 pints) water
250g (9 oz) bananas	Bordeaux yeast and nutrient
800g ($1\frac{3}{4}$ lb) sugar	
15ml (3 teaspoons) citric acid	

Peel and mash the bananas, heat them with the cleaned and crushed elderberries and leave them to cool. Strain the liquid onto the chopped raisins, press and discard the pulp. Mix in the citric acid, pectic enzyme, active yeast and nutrient. After three days, stir in the sugar and continue fermentation. After another five days, strain out, press and discard the raisins, pour the must into a fermentation jar, fit an airlock and ferment out. Siphon the clearing wine into a sterilised storage jar, top up, bung tight, label and store until the wine is bright, then rack again. No Campden tablets are needed. Mature for at least twelve months.

 ## ELDERBERRY DESSERT WINE

900g (2 lb) elderberries, cleaned and crushed
450g (1 lb) blackberries
450g (1 lb) raisins
4 bananas
450g (1 lb) cooking apples
1.25kg (2¾ lb) sugar

15ml (3 teaspoons) citric acid
5ml (1 teaspoon) pectic enzyme
3.7 litres (6½ pints) water
Port yeast and nutrient

In a large pan put the elderberries, blackberries and bananas. Add the water and bring to a temperature of 80°C (175°F) for about 20 minutes until the elderberries 'dimple'. Pour the liquid into a bin containing the washed and chopped raisins. Mix in the citric acid and the pectic enzyme. Crush the apples into pulp and add to the bin, cover and leave for 24 hours.

Add an activated yeast and nutrient and ferment on the pulp for five days, pressing down the fruit cap twice daily. Strain out and press the fruit dry, stir in half the sugar, pour the must into a fermentation jar, fit an airlock and ferment on.

After one week, remove some must, stir in half the remaining sugar and return it to the jar. After another week, add the rest of the sugar. When fermentation finishes, rack into a clean jar, top up, bung tight and store until the wine is bright. Rack again, sweeten to taste if necessary and keep for at least two years.

CRAB APPLE WINE

Crab apple trees are often grown just for their beauty. In spring, they have an abundance of bright-hued flowers, varying from pure white to a purplish red. In summer, they are full of rich green or reddish leaves. In autumn, they carry a harvest of fruits, some as small as red or green marbles, others like small golden eggs tinged with red and still others as large as yellow golf balls or small red billiard balls. The colour season often extends for eight months and gives joy the whole time.

The winemaker, however, can enjoy further pleasure from these generous trees, for the fruits make delicious wine as well as jelly conserve. For the

gardener wishing to plant a crab apple tree, John Downie and Golden Hornet can be as warmly recommended as *Malus Robusta* – both yellow and red varieties. Two others worth looking for are *Malus Floribunda* – the Japanese crab apple – and *Malus Prunifolia*, another of the Siberian crab apples. *Malus Purpurea* is the one with the beautiful purple/red blossom, leaf and tiny fruit. It is not so suitable for wine as the others mentioned. The trees do not grow very large and are suitable for urban roadsides and front gardens.

2.5kg (5½ lb) crab apples
250g (9 oz) concentrated white grape juice
750g (1 lb 10 oz) sugar
5ml (1 teaspoon) citric acid

3 litres (5 pints) water
Pectic enzyme
2 Campden tablets
Champagne yeast and nutrient

Wash, remove the stalks from the apples and crush them. Drop them at once into a bin containing the cold water, citric acid and 1 crushed Campden tablet. Cover and leave in a warm place for 24 hours. Stir in the grape juice, nutrient and the activated yeast, then ferment on the pulp for seven days, keeping the fruit well submerged. Strain out and press the fruit dry; stir in the sugar and pour the must into a fermentation jar, fit an airlock and ferment out. Any surplus must should be fermented in a wine bottle plugged with cotton wool and stood beside the jar.

Rack the young wine into a sterilised jar, top up, add 1 Campden tablet, bung tight, and store until it is bright. Rack into bottles and keep for one year or a little longer.

When autumn sunshine has sweetened the crab apples, they contain a nice balance between acid and sugar, and make a particularly good dry white wine.

Should you be so lucky, however, as to end up with a wine not just to your taste, don't despair. Crab apple wine is excellent for blending. Provided the wine is sound, it will blend well with any other wine, but especially with apples, elderberries, raisins, sultanas, dates and plums.

It might be as well to taste your crab apples before you crush them and if they taste particularly sour, add 15ml (3 teaspoons) of glycerine with the sugar and when the wine is finished and bright, sweeten it with saccharin. I also find that a Sauternes wine yeast is best when the apples are very sour.

If you haven't got enough crab apples to make this wine, add some Worcester Pearmain eating apples and make the total weight up to 2.7kg (6 lb). There is very little colour in the skins of apples and only the faintest tinge of pink can be expected even from red apples. Generally the colour is golden.

MIXED PLUM ROSE

The number of different kinds of plum fruits confuses some people. They wonder which variety makes the best wine and in their lack of confidence miss the market. This recipe is designed not only to help such people but also to make the utmost use of the splendid plum crop.

All the different varieties make wine, Victoria plum being especially good for making into a sherry type. But this apart, no one variety makes as good a wine on its own as in conjunction with others. If your fruiterer has a wide selection of cherry plums, greengages, golden plums, black plums and so on, buy a few of each variety available, whether cooking or dessert. Assemble together at least four different varieties of plums.

Occasionally, plum wines develop a sort of bloom or sheen, due, it is thought, to the waxy bloom of the fruit. If your plums have a somewhat greasy feel, wash them in hot water containing a little washing soda and then rinse them in clean water before cutting them to remove the stones. It is always most important to remove and discard every stone otherwise the wine might become unpleasantly tainted.

The blending of the different varieties brings out the best of them all and makes such a good wine that it is worth making double the quantity than the 5 litres (1 gallon) made in this recipe. Increase the quantities of all the ingredients *pro rata* except the yeast, but make a bigger starter and give it an extra 24 hours to develop a larger colony.

2kg (4½ lb) mixed plums	4 litres (7 pints) water
2 ripe bananas	Pectic enzyme
175g (6 oz) sultanas	2 Campden tablets
800g (1¾ lb) sugar	Bordeaux wine yeast and
5ml (1 teaspoon) citric acid	nutrient
2.5ml (½ teaspoon) grape tannin	

Wash and stalk the plums, halve them and remove the stones, then drop them at once into a bin of hot water in which the citric acid has been dissolved. Peel and thinly slice the bananas and add them to the bin, as well as the washed and chopped sultanas. Cover the bin and leave the mash to cool.

Add the pectic enzyme, tannin, and 1 crushed Campden tablet, cover the bin and leave for 24 hours. Next day add the activated wine yeast and nutrient and ferment on the pulp for only three days, keeping the pulp well submerged with a plate.

Strain out and gently press the pulp, stir in the sugar, pour the must into a fermentation jar, fit an airlock and ferment out. Move the wine to a cool place and rack the wine from its lees after two or three days. Add 1 Campden tablet and store for two months, rack again and store for six months, then bottle and keep for a few months longer.

The colour of this wine varies from a rosé to a light red, depending on the plums used. The bouquet is fresh and fruity and the flavour is clean and attractively vinous. The wine is dry but may be sweetened to taste when serving.

Serve plum wine with cold meats and salads, with veal, poultry, rabbit or with a mild cheese like Caerphilly. Sometimes, plum wine tastes better cool than at room temperature and it is worth an experiment to find the best for your wine.

October

This is really the best month for making elderberry and sloe wines as well as home-grown grape wine. The elderberries can be seen to ripen and hang heavily in their drupes – if other winemakers and the birds haven't got them first. This is a dilemma I face every year. Late-gathered elderberries certainly make superb wine and are worth picking if you can find them and reach them – for they are usually left because other pickers could not reach them. Similarly with sloes which benefit from a frost. If you know of some likely to catch an early frost, then tell no one, but leave them as late as you can for the choicest sloe wine – or gin!

Grapes, too, should be watched carefully. They should have been covered with netting way back in July to protect them from the birds. Keep an eye on both the grapes and the weather. If it turns wet and cold, gather them in as soon as you can before they turn mouldy. If it keeps fine and dry, leave them until the leaves drop.

Italian wine grapes are becoming easier to find in this country. Syndicates exist bringing container loads from Italy. It is not difficult to buy a share. The large Italian colony in London bring over truck loads of grapes and make their own wine. Very good it is too, for I have been privileged to taste the finished wine.

You need about 8kg (18 lb) of grapes to make six bottles of wine. Remove the main stalk, crush the grapes by hand (or by foot!), mix in a Chianti-style wine yeast and ferment on the pulp for from ten to fourteen days before straining and pressing. Mix up the pulp in the straining bag several times and then renew the pressing. I never cease to marvel at how much extra juice comes out as a result. Even when I can get no more juice out of the cake of skins and pips, I never discard it without first adding it to some other wine that I am fermenting on the pulp. The residue contains tannins, colour and mineral traces beneficial to home-made wines.

Hop gathering in the 1790s

ROSEHIP WINE

There are few sights more exciting in the autumn than a large wild rose bush aflame with orange hips. You often come across them when out looking for elderberries or sloes. Like sloes and parsnips, they are thought by old country people to be at their best after the first frost. It depends on how soon the first frost comes and who gets there first, hungry birds or other winemakers. My advice is to gather them when you can. Pick the most orange hips, leaving those that have become soft and tinged with brown. Often they grow in threes which speeds up the picking but do remember the thorns and either wear leather gloves or be prepared for scratches.

You need quite a lot of fresh hips to make even 5 litres (1 gallon) of wine, so pick away until you have become bored or fed up. It helps enormously if you have a companion to help you.

When you get them home, top and tail them with a sharp knife and wash them in running cold water. I never cease to be surprised at how dirty they are when they look so good. I then drain them and shake off all the surplus water, pack them into a polythene bag and freeze them until I have time to make the wine. This recipe is for a sweet table wine.

1.8kg (4 lb) rosehips	3 Campden tablets
250g (9 oz) sultanas	3.4 litres (6 pints) water
1kg (2¼ lb) sugar	Sauternes yeast and
15ml (3 teaspoons) citric acid	nutrient
2.5ml (½ teaspoon) grape tannin	1g (⅕ teaspoon) potassium sorbate (Sorbistat)
5ml (1 teaspoon) pectic enzyme	

Thaw and crush the frozen hips, pour boiling water over them, cover and leave to cool. Wash and chop the sultanas and add to the rosehips, together with the citric acid, pectic enzyme and 1 crushed Campden tablet. Leave for 24 hours. Add the yeast nutrient and tannin and ferment on the pulp for five days, keeping the fruit submerged and the bin covered. Strain out, press dry and discard the fruit, stir in the sugar, pour the must into a fermentation jar, top up with cold boiled water, fit an airlock and ferment down to a specific gravity of 1.016.

Siphon the wine into a clean jar containing one gram potassium sorbate and 1 crushed Campden tablet. Bung tight and stand the jar in a cold place to encourage the sediment to settle.

Rack again when the wine is bright, add 1 more crushed Campden tablet and store the wine in a cool place for nine months. Bottle and store for a further six months. Serve this sweet table wine chilled with the dessert course of a meal, or with sweet biscuits.

ENGLISH GRAPE WINE

I have been surprised to learn from various sources, just how many people now grow a few vines in their gardens. Alas, most of them will not make very good wine because almost no grape variety makes really good wine on its own. A blend of grapes is essential. If you only have the one vine do try to find room to plant some others this autumn. White grape varieties do best in England because in most years we don't get enough sunshine to ripen the black grapes properly. But one black vine among several whites is sufficient to produce a rosé wine.

The vines need watching almost daily just now. Assuming that you have protected them from the birds, leave the grapes as long as you can on the vines. If your local weather turns damp and miserable, however, gather the grapes before they spoil. The moisture attracts the wild yeasts, bacteria and moulds, and the grapes soon rot; and it isn't likely to be the 'noble rot' that makes Sauternes so delicious!

Once gathered, remove the centre stalk and side stems and crush each berry. If they are a bit mouldy and you have a pan large enough, place them in it and raise the temperature to 80°C (175°F) for 5 minutes. If this is not possible, then be content with sulphite at the rate of 100 p.p.m., i.e. 2 Campden tablets per 5 litres (1 gallon) of must. If the grapes are all perfect then one tablet is enough, but don't omit it and try to rely on the bloom to ferment the must. No professional winemaker takes such a risk and neither should you. Also add 5ml (1 teaspoon) of a pectin-destroying enzyme per 5 litres (1 gallon). This improves the extraction and assists with the clarification of the finished wine. Cover the must and leave it for 24 hours in a warm place.

White grapes should now be pressed as hard as possible. The sugar content of the juice should be checked with a hydrometer. A minimum reading of 1.074 is needed to produce an alcohol content of 10%. Some of the German wines have a specific gravity as low as 1.066 but that makes only an everyday wine. You can add some ordinary white sugar to increase the reading and 56g (2 oz) will increase the reading by about 5 points in 5 litres (1 gallon) of must. Take out some of the juice, dissolve the sugar in it and return it to the bulk. The juice should now be inoculated with a German wine yeast such as Hock, Mosel or Johannisberg, and fermented under an airlock in a coolish temperature of around 15°C (60°F).

The juice of black grapes should be similarly checked and, if necessary, increased to a minimum of specific gravity 1.080 and a maximum of 1.090. The black grapes should be sulphited and treated with enzyme for 24 hours before the yeast is added – a Burgundy wine yeast has been found to be the best for English black grapes. The skins, pulp, pips and juice are fermented together for a week to ten days until the colour of the wine is as dark as you want it to be. The solids are then strained out and pressed so that the fermentation can be continued under an airlock. All the while the must is being fermented on the pulp, the fruit should be kept submerged with a weighted plate or by pressing down the cap with a wooden spoon twice a day. Otherwise the cap dries out and becomes a breeding ground for spoilage organisms.

When fermentation of the white or the red wine has finished, rack the wine from its sediment, add 1 Campden tablet per 5 litres (1 gallon) and leave the wine in a cool place to clear. Rack again and keep the white wine until next May before bottling it, and the red wine until next October.

SLOE WINE

The sloe is an egg-shaped, blue-black berry about the size of a small grape, growing singly on the branches of a hedgerow shrub, protected with fierce thorns about 3cm (1 in) long. It is best to gather them after a frost or two when the sugar has been concentrated. The sloes should then be soft to the touch, devoid of any green hue and easily removed from their stalk.

Sloes may be used to make either a table wine or a dessert wine or, with gin, an interesting liqueur. The fruit blends well with the rest of the autumn harvest.

1.35kg (3 lb) sloes
2 ripe bananas
250g (9 oz) concentrated
*   red grape juice*
10ml (2 teaspoons) citric
*   acid*
2.5ml ($\frac{1}{2}$ teaspoon) grape
*   tannin*

750g (1 lb 10 oz) sugar
4 litres (7 pints) water
1 Campden tablet
Burgundy wine yeast and
*   nutrient*

Remove any stalks from the sloes and rinse them in cold water. Place them in a large boiling pan with 2.3 litres (4 pints) water. Peel the bananas, cut them into small pieces and add them to the sloes. Place the pan on a stove and heat slowly to 80°C (175°F). Maintain this temperature for 15 minutes, then leave to cool.

Meanwhile, place the sugar in another pan, add the citric acid and 1.2 litres (2 pints) of water. Bring to the boil, stirring to dissolve the sugar, and simmer gently for 20 minutes, then leave to cool.

Strain the liquid into a fermentation jar, press the fruit gently, then discard it. Add the concentrated grape juice, the sugar syrup, the grape tannin and the activated yeast; top up, fit an airlock and ferment out in a warm place, 20°C (68°F). As soon as the wine begins to clear, siphon it into a clean jar and discard the sediment. Top up, add 1 Campden tablet and store for eight or nine months before bottling.

This wine is ready for drinking one year from making. Serve it at room temperature.

ROWANBERRY WINE

These brilliant red berries, hanging in great clusters amidst bright green leaves, are a source of temptation to the winemaker, the more so since the berries are for free! In some places the tree is called the mountain ash. The berries are used for cattle food as well as for making into a fruit jelly. They have been widely used for flavouring beer as well as for making into wine. But the flavour is somewhat bitter and rowanberries are best used in moderation and in conjunction with other ingredients.

The various stages of making wine as drawn by a French school manual

900g (2 lb) ripe rowanberries	5ml (1 teaspoon) citric acid
450g (1 lb) ripe rosehips	4 litres (7 pints) water
2 ripe bananas	Pectic enzyme
225g ($\frac{1}{2}$ lb) raisins	2 Campden tablets
1 fresh lemon	Wine yeast and nutrient
800g (1$\frac{3}{4}$ lb) sugar	

Stalk and wash the rowanberries and rosehips, then crush them with a rolling pin just enough to open them. Place them in a large pan with the thinly pared lemon skin, the peeled and thinly sliced bananas and the water. Bring to a temperature of 80°C (175°F) and hold this for half an hour, keeping the pan covered the whole time so as not to lose volatile flavours in the steam. It is important not to boil the berries and hips so as not to extract too much bitterness. But it is necessary to steep them in very hot water for half an hour to extract the soluble nutrients.

Strain the hot liquid onto the washed and chopped raisins, discard the berries and hips, cover the bin and leave to cool.

Squeeze the juice from the lemon. Add the acid, the strained lemon juice, pectic enzyme and 1 Campden tablet. Top up with cold water to 4.3 litres (7$\frac{1}{2}$ pints), cover and leave for 24 hours. Next day, add an actively fermenting wine yeast and ferment the raisins on the pulp for four days, keeping them submerged or pressed down. Strain out and press the raisins dry, stir in the sugar, pour the must into a fermentation jar, fit an airlock and ferment out.

Move the wine to a cool place for a few days, then rack it from its lees, top up and add 1 Campden

tablet. Bung the jar tight, label and store until the wine is bright, then rack again.

Rowanberry wine needs at least a year to mature and lose the harshness of its flavour. When it is mature, it tastes very smooth and round, and has a good bouquet as well. If you think that it tastes too dry, then sweeten it to suit your palate just prior to serving it. It is best served cool as an apéritif with crisps and peanuts.

SPARKLING PEAR WINE

A well-known and deservedly popular sparkling wine is made in Somerset from pears. Home wine-makers can make a very acceptable imitation at a fraction of the price if they take the trouble.

3kg (6$\frac{1}{2}$ lb) hard pears	2 Campden tablets
250g (9 oz) concentrated white grape juice	3 litres (5$\frac{1}{4}$ pints) cold water
800g (1$\frac{3}{4}$ lb) sugar	Champagne wine yeast and nutrient
15ml (3 teaspoons) citric acid	Saccharin tablets
Pectic enzyme	

Put the cold water in a large bin, add the citric acid, 1 Campden tablet and the pectic enzyme. Wash the pears, cut them into small pieces or crush them. Add them to the bin. Cover and leave for 24 hours. Next day add the concentrated grape juice, an activated Champagne wine yeast and the nutrient. Ferment on the pulp for five days, keeping the pulp submerged the whole time.

Strain out and press the pulp dry, stir in the sugar and pour the must into a fermentation jar. Fit an airlock and ferment out to dryness. An extra 2.5ml ($\frac{1}{2}$ teaspoon) of nutrient will ensure this.

When fermentation is finished, move the jar to a cool place or leave it out of doors for a couple of nights, to encourage the sediment to settle. Rack into a clean jar, top up, add 1 Campden tablet and store until the wine is crystal bright. If this has not happened after four weeks, add a fining agent, rack again as soon as the wine is bright but do not add any more Campden tablets.

Store the wine for six months, then pour it into a clean bin so that it can take up some oxygen from the air. Stir in another newly activated Champagne wine yeast and nutrient and 70g ($2\frac{1}{2}$ oz) of caster sugar. This quantity is critical and must be measured accurately.

Siphon the wine into six sterilised Champagne bottles – no others are suitable and could be dangerous. Fill them to within 5cm (2 in) of the top so leaving essential space for the pressure of carbon dioxide. Seal the bottles with hollow-domed, plastic stoppers and fasten them on with wire cages. Store the bottles on their sides for seven days in a warm place. This is important for the secondary fermentation. Store the bottles for at least six months in a cool place while the wine matures. Longer is preferable.

Up-end the bottles and each day give them a slight knock and twist to encourage the sediment to move from the side of the bottle into the hollow dome of the stopper. A few days in the boot of a car while driving round town does wonders in this respect.

When the sediment has settled and the wine is quite clear, chill the bottles in the refrigerator, then place the stopper and neck of each bottle in a bowl of crushed ice to which 15ml (3 teaspoons) of cooking salt have been added. After 10 minutes, the wine in the stopper will be frozen. Stand the bottle upright without shaking it, remove the cage and stopper, quickly sweeten the wine to your taste with one or two saccharin tablets per bottle and fit a clean and softened stopper and cage as fast as you can. Keep the wine until it is required and serve it nicely chilled.

APPLE AND GOOSEBERRY WINE

In spite of each autumn's fears for the apple crop, there is usually a good supply of apples about, especially of Bramleys, Blenheims and Laxtons. Canned and frozen gooseberries are also available. This wine is one that I made from a surplus of frozen apples and gooseberries. Freezing or canning fruit seems in some

Autumn by F. Walker, 1865

way to speed up the maturing process, and wines made from ingredients that have been canned or frozen seem to mature more quickly than similar wines made from fresh fruits.

This apple and gooseberry wine matured within three or four months and had that fresh, crispy flavour of a Moselle wine. My one regret was that there was not enough of it.

1.6kg ($3\frac{1}{2}$ lb) Blenheim apples	5ml (1 teaspoon) citric acid
1kg ($2\frac{1}{4}$ lb) Laxton or Cox's apples	5ml (1 teaspoon) pectic enzyme
450g (1 lb) canned or frozen gooseberries	2 Campden tablets
250g (9 oz) concentrated white grape juice	2.3 litres (4 pints) water
750g (1 lb 10 oz) sugar	German wine yeast and nutrient

Wash and crush the apples and drop them at once into a bin containing 2.3 litres (4 pints) of cold water, 1 crushed Campden tablet, the pectic enzyme and the citric acid. Crush the gooseberries, add these to the bin, cover and leave it for 24 hours.

Next day, add the concentrated grape juice and an active yeast and nutrient. Ferment on the pulp for five days, keeping the fruit submerged the whole time. Strain out and press the pulp dry, stir in the sugar, pour the must into a fermentation jar, top up with cold water, fit an airlock and ferment out. A room temperature of 15°C (60°F) gives better results with this wine than a higher one, but fermentation takes a little longer to complete.

When fermentation is finished, rack as usual, add 1 Campden tablet and store in a cool place until the wine is bright, then bottle and keep the wine for a few weeks longer. Finings may be added at the first racking to speed up the precipitation of the solids, although the wine usually clears naturally.

Serve the wine cold as a white table wine. If it isn't sweet enough, dissolve 1 or 2 saccharin tablets in each bottle of wine.

Apples make a splendid base for a variety of wines. Using the same recipe, substitute 450g (1 lb) canned or frozen blackberries, raspberries or loganberries and a Bordeaux yeast instead of a German one. A light rosé wine is produced that would be ready for drinking on summer picnics. Experience shows that imported apples from Italy, France and Tasmania, although delightful in themselves, are not so suitable for making wine as home-grown English apples. The resulting wine lacks 'character'.

SCRUMPY CIDER

After an autumn storm with strong winds, those of us with a few apple trees in our gardens often find that the apples are lying all around us. Although none of mine are the proper cider apples, I can still make a worthwhile 'scrumpy'.

Use the widest mixture of apples that you can get. Windfalls may be used, but they must be cleaned up first and only unbruised fruit should be crushed.

You need a press of some sort. A small purpose-made press solves the problem completely, but they are expensive for a one-off use. Members of wine-making clubs may have access to one bought by the club for lending out.

Crushing the apples prior to pressing is less of a problem and two methods have been described in the recipe for Olde English Cider on page 72. Another way is to cut the apples into quarters or eighths, dropping them into a sulphite solution as you do so. Strain them out, pack them in polythene bags and freeze them for two days or more. Upon removal and thawing they will be soft and can be easily crushed in their bag, then emptied into the press bag.

The crushed fruit is placed in a sterilised hessian or nylon bag before being pressed. As the juice flows out, make sure that you have a suitable bin or bucket in which to collect it. Polythene sheeting or split polythene bags can be placed around the press to ensure that the juice doesn't squirt everywhere but in the bin. Before you start, get your press and collecting bin well organised. The pressing is not hard work. The two-handed screw sees to that. But it does need thoughtful improvisation, and everyone must solve this problem in the best manner suggested by the

materials and equipment that they have most readily available. Temporary bins can be improvised from strong, liquid-proof polythene bags, supported by cardboard cartons. Secure the neck with a rubber band. Whilst suitable for fermenting and racking, polythene bags are not suitable for storage of scrumpy because they are not vapour proof.

Unless you are going to make several gallons of scrumpy, it is hardly worth the trouble. But the effort is not much in relation to the result if you have plenty of apples that would otherwise be wasted. This recipe makes 18 litres (4 gallons).

36kg (80 lb) assorted mellow apples
1kg (2¼ lb) cider concentrate
Sugar as necessary
20ml (4 teaspoons) pectic enzyme
4 Campden tablets
Champagne wine yeast

Crush and press the apples, stirring up the pulp from time to time in the press. Dissolve the cider concentrate in the pressed apple juice and measure the gravity of the must with a hydrometer. You should have at least 18 litres (4 gallons) of must, depending on how well you have crushed and pressed your fruit. The gravity should be somewhere between 1.030 and 1.060, varying with the sweetness of the apples. Add sufficient sugar, if necessary, to increase the gravity to 1.048. 225g (8 oz) of sugar will raise the reading in 18 litres (4 gallons) by about four points.

Take out 575ml (1 pint) of juice, add 275ml (½ pint) of warm water, pour it into a bottle, add the yeast, plug the neck of the bottle with cotton wool or a paper tissue, and stand it in a warm place – 40°C (104°F). Shake it every now and then to encourage the take-up of oxygen from the air. Meanwhile, add pectic enzyme and 4 crushed Campden tablets to the bulk juice, cover and leave it for 24 hours.

When the yeast starter is fermenting vigorously – usually after 24 hours – stir it into the bulk of the juice. Replace the cover and ferment in the bin for three days. The cider must should now be poured into sterilised jars and airlocks fitted, but it may be left in its bin and kept well covered, although with facility for the gas to escape. Ferment slowly in a cool place, 15°C (60°F), to a specific gravity of 1.002. Siphon into sterilised beer bottles, seal securely and mature for six months. Serve the scrumpy cool.

The scrumpy should be a golden yellow with an appley aroma, dry on the palate, but with a lively effervescence when poured. If you want it sweet, add 1 saccharin tablet per 575ml (1 pint). For a still cider, continue fermentation to a finish in the jar or bin, rack it into a sterilised jar and add 1 Campden tablet per 5 litres (1 gallon). If it remains hazy, add 30ml (2 tablespoons) of fresh milk, shake it up well, then leave it to settle in the cool, say outside one night. As soon as it is bright, rack it again.

November

At this time of year it is important to keep an eye open for loose-fitting bungs. Sometimes the cork shrinks as it dries and consequently permits air to enter the jar. Push all corks home as tight as possible and at all times make sure that the jars are well filled and securely sealed. If an air space is left in any but a sherry-style wine, the wine could become over-oxidised and develop a taint. If, in addition, the jar is insecurely sealed, a fungus called *mycoderma vini* or flowers of wine could enter the jar. It will grow on the surface of the wine in the presence of oxygen and form a creamy white film. Such a film seen in a jar should receive immediate attention, for the fungus will gradually convert all the alcohol into water!

The easiest way to remove the film is to float it off. Very carefully add a similar wine or even cold boiled water to the jar, slowly raising the level until it reaches the mouth of the jar. A few drops more, then a slight tilt of the jar and the film will float over the edge. Remove sufficient wine to get a bung into the jar, then add 2 Campden tablets per 5 litres (1 gallon), fit a freshly sterilised and softened bung and push it home as tight as you can. It helps to place a piece of sterilised string or plastic-coated wire into the neck of the jar just before you push the bung home. When the bung is securely in place, withdraw the string or plastic-coated wire, thus releasing some of the air pressure beneath the bung. This will ensure the retention of the tight fit and prevent further infection.

A busy stable by J. F. Herring Senior

When the must is cool, stir in the concentrated grape juice, the lemon juice, tartaric acid, tannin and an activated yeast and nutrient. Pour the must into a fermentation jar, fit an airlock, tie on a label and leave the jar not quite full in a warm place for seven days. Stir in 225g ($\frac{1}{2}$ lb) sugar and continue to add 225g ($\frac{1}{2}$ lb) sugar each week until it has all been added.

When fermentation finishes, siphon the clearing wine into a clean jar. Taste the wine and if it is not sweet enough add sufficient sugar to sweeten it to your taste. Fit a safety bung and store the wine in a cool place.

As soon as the wine is star bright, siphon it from the new sediment into a storage jar; then bung, label and store until this time next year. Bottle the wine and keep it for another six months or so. Serve it at room temperature with cheese and nuts, cheese and apple or fruit cake.

CARROT WINE

When the humble carrot costs 30p per lb in May, it becomes a luxury in many households. Now that the maincrop is in the shops or ready for digging in the garden, the opportunity should be taken to use some to make this very interesting wine. Use the carrot as soon as it is fully grown, preferably when it still has the tangy flavour of the freshness of a 'spring' carrot.

2kg (4$\frac{1}{2}$ lb) carrots	2.5ml ($\frac{1}{2}$ teaspoon) grape
500g (18 oz) concentrated	tannin
white grape juice	3.4 litres (6 pints) water
1.25kg (2$\frac{3}{4}$ lb) sugar	Tokay yeast and nutrient
10ml (2 teaspoons) citric	
acid	

Cut off the tap root and the foliage of the carrots and then scrub them free from every vestige of soil. Dice them and place them in a boiling pan with 2.3 litres (4 pints) of water. Bring them to the boil and simmer them for about half an hour until they are soft and tender, but not mushy. Leave them to cool, then strain off but do not press the carrots. If you wish you may use them as a vegetable. To the carrot liquid stir in the concentrated white grape juice, the citric acid, grape tannin, yeast and nutrient. Mix them all together, fit an airlock and leave the jar in a warm place. Check the specific gravity and as soon as it falls to 1.006, take out some wine and dissolve 450g (1 lb) sugar in it. Return it to the jar, replace the airlock and continue the fermentation. Repeat this process again with half the remaining sugar and a third time with the rest. Top up with cold boiled water and ferment out.

When fermentation finally stops, check the specific gravity and, if necessary, add sufficient

BEETROOT DESSERT WINE

The great attraction of beetroot for making wine is the wonderful red of its juice. For this reason it is mostly made into a sweet and strong dessert wine reminiscent of port. The one disadvantage appears to be what some people describe as an 'earthy' taste. With proper preparation this danger can be averted.

Use fresh mature beets that are not too large, top and tail them and scrub them really clean and free from every trace of soil and blemished skin. The skin needs quite a hard brushing, not just a gentle wash.

2kg (4$\frac{1}{2}$ lb) diced beetroot	10ml (2 teaspoons)
500g (18 oz) concentrated	tartaric acid
red grape juice	5ml (1 teaspoon) grape
4 bananas	tannin
1.25kg (2$\frac{3}{4}$ lb) sugar	3.5 litres (6 pints) water
7g ($\frac{1}{4}$ oz) fresh root ginger	Port wine yeast and
12 whole cloves	nutrient
1 lemon	

Dice the beetroot and put into a pan, together with the peeled and sliced bananas, the thinly pared lemon rind, the grated ginger and cloves. Bring to the boil and cook until they are tender – about 30 minutes. Strain the beetroot liquid into a mashing bin and cover. Squeeze the juice from the lemon.

sugar to increase the reading of 1.016. Move the jar to a cool place for a week to clear most of the sediment from the wine, then siphon it into a clean jar, top up, bung tight, label and store.

Keep the wine in a cool place until it is bright, then rack again and keep for two years. This strong sweet wine with a most distinctive flavour should be served as an after-dinner dessert wine in a fairly small glass. Serve it cool rather than cold – just below room temperature is best.

The Tokay flavour can be enhanced by pouring the hot carrot liquid on to 450g (1 lb) sultanas. Omit the grape juice concentrate. Ferment the sultanas in a bin for ten days, remove them and squeeze them dry before discarding them. Then add the sugar.

MARROW WINE

Because of our wet and occasionally warm summers, marrows are usually plentiful and cheap at this time of year. The profusion of marrows and pumpkins frequently tempts people into making wine from them and I have often been asked for a recipe. Although the marrow has plenty of thin juice, its slight flavour doesn't come through into the finished wine successfully and it is necessary to add a spice or two of your choice. If you are in an 'experimental' mood, try this recipe with either marrow or pumpkin.

2.5–3kg (5½–6½ lb) marrow	2 lemons
500g (18 oz) sultanas	2.5ml (½ teaspoon) grape tannin
675g (1½ lb) sugar	4 litres (7 pints) water
5ml (1 teaspoon) malic acid	Pectic enzyme
30g (1 oz) root ginger	Campden tablets
12 cloves	All-purpose wine yeast and nutrient

Wash the marrow clean, cut off and discard the stump, then cut the marrow up into small cubes. Be careful not to cut the seeds, as they would impart an unpleasant taste but they should be included with the pulp and skin. Pare the rind from the lemons, squeeze the juice and strain it. Wash and chop the sultanas and bruise the ginger roots. Place the marrow in a fermentation bin together with the lemon rind, the lemon juice, the sultanas, the ginger roots, cloves, malic acid, tannin, pectic enzyme and 1 crushed Campden tablet. Pour on the water, cover and leave in a warm place for 24 hours. Next day, add an actively fermenting wine yeast and nutrient, cover and ferment on the pulp for four days, keeping the pulp submerged with a china plate.

Strain out and press the pulp, stir in the sugar, pour the must into a fermentation jar, fit an airlock and ferment out. Move the jar to a cool place for a couple of days, then rack the clearing wine from its sediment and store it until it is bright. Rack again, into bottles if you so wish, and mature this young wine for six months.

This is a dry white wine that should be served well chilled especially with any fish, pork or poultry dish.

You will notice that the quantity of spices used is quite small so that their flavour will be subtle rather than dominant. Be careful not to overdo them. The sugar quantity is small because there is 350g (12 oz) fermentable sugar already in the sultanas – a point that is often overlooked. The wine will have an alcohol content of around 11% – an adequate amount for the flavour and body. It would be unwise to add more sugar. If you prefer a sweeter wine, then sweeten it to suit your taste with saccharin or lactose.

DRIED APRICOT WINE

After the grape, one of the best fruits for winemaking must surely be the apricot, with the gooseberry a close third. Not only do fresh apricots make a superb light white wine of Muscadet style, but also the dried fruit, the canned fruit and the fruit juice all make excellent wines. The dried fruit, too, is a splendid additive to many other wines to improve the bouquet, the flavour and the body. At this time of year, dried apricots, canned apricots and apricot 'nectar' are all available for making wine.

Health food shops sell two varieties of dried apricots, pitted whole apricots and, at about half the price, apricot pieces. The pieces are excellent for winemaking. Some wholesalers also sell them in a 3kg (6¾ lb) polythene bag. The dried fruit is equal to four times its weight in fresh fruit and so very little is required. The flavour is enhanced in the drying process and 350–450g (¾–1 lb) of dried apricot pieces is enough for 5 litres (1 gallon) of wine.

350g (12 oz) dried apricots	4 litres (7 pints) water
2 ripe bananas	Pectic enzyme
250g (9 oz) concentrated white grape juice	1 Campden tablet
800g (1¾ lb) sugar	All-purpose wine yeast and nutrient
15ml (3 teaspoons) citric acid	

Rinse the apricot pieces in a light sulphite solution, chop them up, place them in a bowl, cover them with hot water, then a lid and leave them to soak overnight. Empty the swollen apricot pieces and liquid into a large pan, add the peeled and thinly sliced bananas together with 1.2 litres (2 pints) of water. Raise the temperature to 80°C (175°F) and maintain

Mix together the fruit juice, the grape juice and the water, stir in the citric acid, the pectic enzyme and an activated yeast. Pour the must into a demijohn, fit an airlock and ferment for one week. Remove a third of the must, stir in half the sugar, return it to the jar, replace the airlock and continue the fermentation.

One week later, repeat the process with the rest of the sugar, top up and ferment to a finish. Siphon the clearing wine into a sterilised jar, top up, add 1 Campden tablet, bung tight, label and store in a cool dark place until the wine is bright.

Rack again, this time into bottles, sweeten to taste with saccharin, cork, label and keep until the wine is six months old. Serve the wine nicely chilled.

CANNED APRICOT WINE

Canned apricots also make an excellent wine. The wine matures quickly and is best drunk young and fresh. Made now it would be ready for drinking by the end of July. I prefer apricot pulp to the halves because I fancy that I get more apricots and less syrup. Sometimes these can be obtained from wholesalers in 3kg (6¾ lb) and 6kg (13½ lb) cans and are well worth seeking out. A 3kg (6¾ lb) can makes 23 litres (5 gallons) – thirty bottles – of a superb wine that will see some families through the summer. Smaller quantities may be made but do not last as long. Served really cold in a warm spell of weather, 5 litres (1 gallon) will last a family of four no more than one week, and all they get is two small glasses a day! This wine should therefore be made in as large a quantity as you can. This recipe makes thirty bottles. For sixty bottles (46 litres/10 gallons), just double every item. The 23-litre (5-gallon) plastic containers in cardboard cartons in which bulk sherry is sometimes sold make ideal fermentation and storage vessels for this wine.

this for 20 minutes. Be careful not to boil the fruit. Leave the pan covered while the contents cool.

Strain out the pulp, swirl it round in a sieve or nylon straining bag, and then discard it. Mix in the pectic enzyme, concentrated grape juice, sugar, acid, yeast and nutrient. Pour the must into a demijohn, fit an airlock and ferment to dryness. Rack into a storage jar, top up, add 1 Campden tablet, bung tight, label and store in a cold place until the wine is bright.

Rack again, mature in bulk for six months, then bottle and keep for a further six months. Serve as a dry white table wine or sweeten to taste and serve with sweet biscuits.

APRICOT NECTAR

It is always good to keep in stock a few ingredients for making wine when the mood takes you. Dried fruit, canned fruit and concentrated grape juice are obvious examples but here is a suggestion for a rather exotic wine. Some supermarkets and superior grocers sell bottles of apricot nectar. The bottles usually contain about 600ml, just over (1 pint), and the flavour is so strong that this is enough – with other ingredients – to make six bottles of wine. The wine finishes with a magnificent bouquet and flavour comparable with the bouquet and flavour of a good muscat wine.

1 bottle apricot nectar
500g (18 oz) concentrated white grape juice
500g (18 oz) sugar
5ml (1 teaspoon) citric acid
5ml (1 teaspoon) pectic enzyme
3 litres (5½ pints) water
All-purpose wine yeast and nutrient
1 Campden tablet

3kg (6¾ lb) apricot pieces in syrup
1kg (2¼ lb) ripe bananas
1kg (2¼ lb) concentrated white grape juice
60g (2 oz) citric acid
5ml (1 teaspoon) grape tannin
30g (1 oz) pectic enzyme
3.5kg (7½ lb) white sugar
20 litres (35 pints) water
Hock yeast and nutrient
7 Campden tablets

Open the can of apricots, strain off and store the syrup and crush the apricots with a potato masher, fork or liquidiser. Peel the bananas and do the same to them. Place the fruit in a bin with 9 litres (2 gallons) of cold water, the pectic enzyme, half the acid and 2 crushed Campden tablets. Leave, covered, for 24 hours.

Mix in the concentrated grape juice, the apricot syrup, the tannin, yeast and nutrient and ferment on the pulp for three days, keeping the fruit submerged and the bin covered. Boil the sugar and the rest of the acid in 2.3 litres (4 pints) of water for 20 minutes and leave to cool.

Strain out the fruit pulp through a fine nylon sieve or straining bag, drain it as much as you can, but do not press it. Stir in the sugar syrup, pour the must into an ex-sherry container, top up with cold water, screw on the cap and tap. Turn the cap to open and plug the outlet with cotton wool.

Ferment out to dryness. Rack into another container, add 5 Campden tablets, screw on the cap and tap, turn this to off and turn the container into the tap downward position. Leave the wine in a cool place until it is three months old, then decant into bottles or one-gallon 'Winemaids'. Keep this in the refrigerator so that the wine is always ready for serving. If the wine is too dry for your palate, sweeten it slightly with saccharin.

OLDE ENGLISHE CIDER

The pleasures of cider have long been known in this country and, indeed, wherever apples are grown. In the seventeenth century, cider from Herefordshire was superior in quality to French white wine. In the countryside it has remained very popular, but urban palates turned to spirits, beer and later 'coke'. In the last ten years or so, there has been a re-awakening of interest in this native beverage, and cider drinking has become popular with many young people. Those with facilities to do so are also turning their hands to making a few gallons.

The best cider is made from special varieties of apples that are often too sharp or too bitter to eat. A blend of apples is always preferred to make a balance between sharpness, bitterness and sweetness. Few of us have access to proper cider apples, but we can make a very palatable cider from other apples if we only think about the ingredients. This recipe makes about 5 litres (1 gallon) of cider.

4.5kg (10 lb) sweet eating apples	*2.3kg (5 lb) crab apples*
	3 Campden tablets
2.3kg (5 lb) sharp cooking apples	*Champagne yeast*

All the apples should be mellow and feel softish, rather than hard. If possible, sound and perfect apples should be used, but windfalls make an acceptable alternative, provided the damaged portions are first removed.

The apples must be washed, crushed, sulphited and pressed as quickly as possible. This is not as easy as one would wish unless you have access to a small press and preferably an apple crusher as well. A stainless-steel blade on the end of an epoxy resin-coated steel shaft that fits into an electric drill makes an ideal crusher and is not expensive to buy. Another way is to place some of the washed apples in a strong plastic bag and to bash them with a mallet!

Crush 2 Campden tablets and add to the pulp to inhibit oxidation. The defect of many commercial as well as amateur-made ciders is their flat taste of oxidised fruit. Modern cider-makers also include 5ml (1 teaspoon) of a pectin-destroying enzyme per 4.5kg (10 lb) apples. However you do it, then, crush the apples as finely as you can, place them in a hessian sack or nylon bag that has been sterilised in sulphite and press them as dry as you possibly can. You may have to open the press and stir up the 'cake' several times before expressing the last 275ml ($\frac{1}{2}$ pint) or so of juice.

Immediately the juice is extracted, add the activated champagne wine yeast. The yeast could be poured into the sterilised jar first and the juice run in straight from the press. Ferment the must under an airlock in a cool room, 15°C (60°F), and when fermentation slows down, rack the young cider from its sediment into a clean jar. Add 1 Campden tablet and store the jar in a cool place from six to eight weeks, until the cider is clear and bright. Bottle the cider in screw-stoppered bottles and keep it for a while longer to mature. Serve it cool and fresh rather than cold.

A sparkling cider may be made in the same way as beer. When it is clear, rack it into beer bottles and prime it with 2.5ml ($\frac{1}{2}$ teaspoon) of caster sugar per 575ml (1 pint). It is not customary to disgorge the sediment but to serve the cider in the same way as beer, being careful not to disturb the sediment.

Making cider

December

The last month of the year is usually a very busy one for winemakers and brewers. The autumn wines need racking, the spring wines need bottling, the days are short and cold. There is little time to do the tasks that you really want to do.

Racking is one of the important tasks that must receive attention. Wine left too long on its lees may develop an unpleasant smell and taste. Do get it off its lees, top it up with a similar style of wine or even water, add 1 Campden tablet per 5 litres (1 gallon) and seal the storage jar tight with a sterilised bung.

If there is no time for bottling, a laminated polythene bag in a cardboard carton makes an ideal home for the wine that is going to be in frequent demand during the month. Known by the – to me – rather unsuitable name of 'Winemaid', the bag has a sensible cap-tap which can be easily removed while the bag in the box is being filled with wine. Replace the cap-tap and the wine is ready for serving by the glass or the carafe. As the wine is removed, the bag collapses on to it, thus excluding air and keeping the wine fresh and unspoiled over several months.

When the bag is empty, remove it from the box, take off the cap-tap, wash the bag out as you would a bottle, sterilise it with a sulphite solution, drain it free from loose moisture, return it to the box and refill the bag with wine. Finally, replace the cap-tap and, once more, you have some wine ready to serve.

HOT DRINKS ON COLD NIGHTS

For all these drinks, use freshly bought spices to ensure their full flavour and fragrance.

Mulled Ale

As a child I can recall seeing my grandfather mull an ale. He sat beside an open fire with a pint mug of strong ale on a stool beside him. He placed the poker in the fire and left it there until the end was red hot. Withdrawing the poker, he tapped it on the hearth to remove loose particles of the fire, then dipped the red hot iron into the ale. A great sizzling followed for a few moments, then the poker was removed and replaced on a stand with the tongs and shovel. The ale was supped and presumably much enjoyed – judging by the look on his face.

With modern central heating few of us have open fires in which to heat a poker. We can, however, heat the beer in a saucepan. Use your strongest ale and do not let it get hotter than 60°C (140°F). If you wish, the ale can be sweetened with treacle or honey, or even flavoured with herbs or spices. A few large chopped raisins and a grating of nutmeg make a start. But this is a drink that calls out for experiment. Look round

the larder and choose those flavourings that you think most appropriate to your palate. The secret is to use very few at first. You can always increase the flavour, but once added, the flavour is there to stay.

Mulled Mead

This, too, is another very old drink. A metheglin can be heated to 60°C (140°F) and is, I think, the best way to enjoy this beverage. A sweet, strong mead can be easily mulled, however, with a large piece of well bruised ginger, or a smaller piece of fresh root ginger grated as you would a carrot. Add a dozen cloves and a small piece of cinnamon bark, say a piece 5cm (2 in) long and 6mm ($\frac{1}{4}$ in) thick. The mull may be sweet enough or may need another tablespoonful of honey.

Mulled Wine

Either red or white wine may be used. Select a wine that is full of body and flavour, strong and sweet. A parsnip and fig Madeira-type, or an elderberry and blackberry Port-type make excellent mulls. Two days before making the mull, grate a piece of fresh ginger root about as big as the first joint of a man's thumb into the wine. Add a dozen cloves and a stick of cinnamon as described for a mulled mead. A tablespoonful of honey, the thinly pared and chopped rind of a lemon and its juice should be added.

Allspice

Stopper the container and leave it in the kitchen until required, but give it a shake now and then. In this way the flavours are more fully extracted. Very slowly heat the wine and its flavourings to 60°C (140°F), then strain it into preheated glasses and serve.

A Winter Wassail

The name of this drink comes from the old English word *waes hael* meaning good health. You can use either a bottle of sweet apple wine or a sweet cider.

First of all, however, select three cooking apples about the size of your fist. Peel each one and grate it into a saucepan containing 75ml (3 fl oz) of the wine or cider. Stir with a wooden spoon to ensure that the apple is coated with the liquor and so prevented from browning. Place the pan on a stove and cook the apple until it is mushy and can be mixed to a smooth paste. Add 85g (3 oz) soft brown sugar, 5ml (1 teaspoon) of powdered ginger and the rest of the apple wine or cider.

Stir well and slowly raise the temperature of the wassail to 60°C (140°F). Add a grating of nutmeg, pour into heated glasses and serve at once.

Traditionally the wassail was poured into a large bowl or loving cup and passed from one to another with the blessing, *Waes hael*. It makes a splendid drink at midnight as you see in the New Year.

SULTANA, THE STANDBY WINE

The main difference between sultanas and raisins is that sultanas are made from small, seedless white grapes while raisins are made from slightly larger blue grapes which may contain pips.

After being picked, the large bunches of white grapes are dipped into hot water containing soda and olive oil. This wrinkles and cracks the skins so that the moisture can begin to evaporate when the grapes are subsequently laid out in the sun. About a week later they are shaken free from the main stalk and graded. Next they are placed in a wire mesh container which is spun quickly round and round to remove the tiny cap stems. They are then washed clean, dried and sprayed with mineral oil to prevent the berries from clumping and to give them an attractive and protective sheen. Finally, they pass slowly through a chamber in which sulphur is being burned to destroy all the micro-organisms.

Before using sultanas for wine, they should be washed in warm water to remove the mineral oil and chopped or minced to lay bare the flesh. The grape sugar is highly concentrated and depending on the quality of the harvest can vary from 50 to 75% of the weight of the fruit. On average, sultanas consist of 66% fermentable sugar and this must always be allowed for when adding them to a must.

One measure of sultanas is equal to four measures of fresh grapes. Between 1.5–2kg (3–4 lb) of sultanas then are needed to make six bottles of wine. They can often be bought in 3kg (7 lb) bags, generally enough for 9 litres (2 gallons) of wine.

3kg (7 lb) chopped sultanas
20ml (4 teaspoons) citric acid
2.5ml ($\frac{1}{2}$ teaspoon) grape tannin
9 litres (2 gallons) water
Hock yeast
1 Campden tablet

Wash and chop the sultanas, place them in a sterilised polythene bin, add the acid and tannin, pour on the water and sprinkle a wine yeast on it. Cover the bin and leave it in a warm place, 21°C (70°F). Each day, press the floating fruit cap back into the water until fermentation is quite finished.

Strain out the sultanas and press them dry. Pour the young wine into a glass jar, top up, add 1 Campden tablet, bung tight and leave it in a cool place until the wine is bright. Rack the wine from its sediment, top up, seal and store for six months before bottling. Serve the wine cold with a sweet biscuit.

This basic recipe may be varied by reducing the water by 25% and fermenting with a Fino sherry yeast, or a Sauternes yeast.

BLACK CHERRY DESSERT WINE

Wandering around the larger supermarkets I never fail to be impressed with the very wide range of food now available. The number of different cheeses that could be served with different wines; the different varieties of dry and savoury biscuits and, above all, the number of different dried fruits and also cans and bottles of different fruits – all of which can be used to make wine.

Of course, some are dearer than others, indeed some are better than others. The Polish range of fruits, including bilberries, are quite superb for making wine. One of my favourite table wines is made from these bottled bilberries, but the black cherries are also to be warmly recommended. It makes a sweetish, full-bodied, wine. Other fruits may be substituted for the cherries if you so wish, but I enjoy the cherry flavour.

440g (15½ oz) can or jar of black cherries
440g (15½ oz) can of prunes in syrup
450g (1 lb) bramble jelly
250g (9 oz) concentrated black grape juice
900g (2 lb) sugar
10ml (2 teaspoons) citric acid
5ml (1 teaspoon) grape tannin
2.8 litres (5 pints) water
Pectic enzyme
1 Campden tablet
Port wine yeast and nutrient

Empty the cherries and prunes into a bin, crush them with a wooden spoon and remove the stones. Add the bramble jelly, the concentrated grape juice, the water, acid, a double dose of pectic enzyme and 1 crushed Campden tablet, cover and leave for 24 hours.

Next day, add an activated wine yeast and ferment on the pulp for three days, keeping the fruit pulp submerged. Strain through a nylon sieve and press the pulp until it is dry. Stir in half the sugar, pour the must into a fermentation jar, leaving room for the rest of the sugar to be added later. Fit an airlock and ferment in a steadily warm place, 21°C (70°F).

After one week, remove some wine, dissolve half the sugar in it and return it slowly to the jar. Replace the airlock on the jar and continue the fermentation for another week. Then add the remaining sugar in the same way.

When fermentation finishes, siphon the clearing wine into a sterilised jar, top up with red wine, bung tight and store in a cool place for a few weeks until the wine is clear. Rack again and store for at least a further six months before bottling. Serve the wine free from chill with a mild cheese, some buttered biscuits and a Cox's Orange Pippin.

BLACKBERRY AND APPLE WINE

Many of us enjoy a glass of red wine, especially with cheese or savoury biscuits. This recipe is for an easy-to-make, quick-maturing, red wine that fits this bill to perfection.

The blackberry part of the wine is provided from canned or bottled blackberries. If you prefer, however, you may use frozen blackberries available from frozen food centres. The apple comes from a carton of unsweetened apple juice that you can buy in most supermarkets. Some red grape juice concentrate improves the vinosity and body of the wine. The result is a pleasing, light red wine, around 11% in alcohol, that matures in about four months. It makes a welcome addition to our wines for late summer drinking about the time when we are picking the fresh apples and blackberries.

1 litre (1¾ pints) unsweetened apple juice
560g (20 oz) blackberries in light syrup
800g (1¾ lb) white sugar
250g (9 oz) concentrated red grape juice
5ml (1 teaspoon) citric acid
5ml (1 teaspoon) grape tannin
Pectic enzyme
2 Campden tablets
2.3 litres (4 pints) water
Burgundy wine yeast and nutrient

Strain off the light syrup from the can of blackberries and store it in a bottle in the refrigerator for future use. Crush the berries with a fork and place them in a mashing bin. Pour the apple juice into the bin, add the water, citric acid, grape tannin, pectic enzyme and 1 crushed Campden tablet. Cover and leave the bin in a warm place for 24 hours, while the enzyme dissolves the pectin in the apple juice and blackberries. Add the concentrated grape juice, the blackberry syrup and an activated wine yeast. Replace the cover and ferment on the pulp for three days, keeping the floating fruit cap submerged.

Strain out, press and discard the blackberries, stir in the sugar, pour the must into a demijohn, fit an airlock and ferment out in a warm place – around 20°C (68°F). When fermentation is finished, move the jar to a cool place to encourage the wine to clear, then rack it into a clean jar, add 1 Campden tablet and store the wine for a few weeks until the wine is bright. If it remains hazy, 15ml (3 teaspoons) of fresh milk works wonders. As soon as the wine is crystal clear, bottle it and keep it for a total of three or four months.

If the wine tastes too dry, add 1 saccharin tablet per bottle. This just takes the edge off the dryness yet doesn't make the wine taste sweet. Serve it free from chill with a main course or with biscuits and cheese.

DRIED ROSEHIPS IN WINE

For those town dwellers who do not have access to the countryside when fresh rosehips are available, dried rosehip shells may be bought in home-brew shops. They may be added to other wines to improve the body and contribute vitamins and trace elements to the yeast. Mixed with other ingredients they make an attractive wine and they are well worth keeping in stock.

I like this recipe which makes a sweet cream sherry-type wine.

250g (9 oz) dried rosehip shells	10ml (2 teaspoons) citric acid
250g (9 oz) dates	2.5ml ($\frac{1}{2}$ teaspoon) grape tannin
900g (2 lb) cooking apples	
250g (9 oz) chopped raisins	1 Campden tablet
	Pectic enzyme
1.25kg (2$\frac{3}{4}$ lb) light brown sugar	Sherry wine yeast and nutrient
4 litres (7 pints) water	

Place the dried rosehips, raisins and dates in a mashing bin and pour hot water over them. Cover and leave to cool. Add the acid, pectic enzyme, 1 Campden tablet and tannin. Then chop and add the apples and leave for 24 hours in a warm place.

Stir in an active yeast. Cover the bin and ferment in a warm place for five days, pressing down the fruit cap twice daily. Count the days from when fermentation can be seen to have started and not from the moment of adding the yeast.

Strain out and press the fruit as dry as you can, stir in half the sugar and continue fermentation in a covered bin rather than in a fermentation jar. After one week, stir in half the remaining sugar, and five days later the final portion.

When fermentation finishes, taste the wine and if it is not sweet enough, stir in a little more sugar. Leave it for a few days in case fermentation starts again, but this is unlikely.

Leave the wine in a cool place for a few days, then siphon the clearing wine from its sediment into a storage jar. The jar should be filled only to the shoulder and the surplus wine should be poured into a litre-size wine bottle. Both should be plugged with cotton wool, labelled and kept in the dark of a cool store.

Rack the wine regularly every three months and within a year to fifteen months the wine will have acquired a distinctive bouquet and flavour that is most attractive. Serve it cool.

QUICK CIDER

Not as many people as would wish have access to sufficient apples to make cider. And of those who have, adequate facilities are not often available. Happily, they can, nevertheless, enjoy a glass of home-brewed cider when they want to, for cider concentrate can quickly and easily be made into an enjoyable cider.

Marketed by several firms, the cider concentrate is available from good home-brew shops and branches of Boots the Chemist. A 1kg (2$\frac{1}{4}$ lb) can containing sufficient concentrate to make 9 litres (2 gallons) of cider is not exactly cheap, but the total cost of making your own cider still works out at about one third the cost of buying the commercial equivalent. The cider is very easy to make.

1kg (2$\frac{1}{4}$ lb) can of cider concentrate	7.25 litres (12$\frac{3}{4}$ pints) cold water
350g (12 oz) sugar	Champagne wine yeast

Sterilise a polythene bin (10-litre/2$\frac{1}{4}$-gallon size) and empty into it the cider concentrate. Wash the tin round with hot water so as not to leave behind any concentrate. Add the sugar to the bin and stir until dissolved. Add the cold water to bring the total

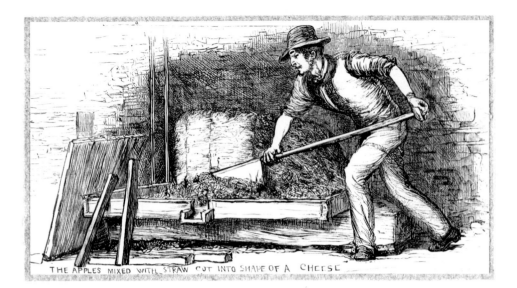

THE APPLES MIXED WITH STRAW CUT INTO SHAPE OF A CHEESE

liquid up to 9 litres (2 gallons) and then stir in the yeast. I use a Champagne yeast but an All-purpose yeast is satisfactory. Fit a lid onto the bin or else pour the must into fermentation jars and fit airlocks. Ferment in a warm place until fermentation is complete.

Check the specific gravity of the must prior to fermentation. I found mine to be 1.046, high enough to produce nearly 6% alcohol. Fermentation takes about ten days. As I like my long drinks to have a little life in them, I bottled my cider with a specific gravity of 1.002. Use proper beer bottles that can withstand the pressure from the carbon dioxide released from the continued fermentation in bottle.

Allow another week for the fermentation to finish before moving the cider to a cool store while it matures. It needs at least one month and will improve still more if left for a further three months.

The colour is clear and an attractive golden-amber, the bouquet is clean and fruity, and the flavour is mild and smooth. My cider contained no trace of the oxidation present in so many ciders that is due to the browning of the apples as they are crushed. This is a fault that could easily be prevented by the proper use of sulphite.

Serve this cider nice and cold and quaff it as a thirst-quencher rather than as a connoisseur's item to be sipped and savoured.

RUSSIAN STOUT

In the heydays of our Baltic trade during the eighteenth and nineteenth centuries, one of our most popular exports was beer. Catherine the Great, the Empress of all the Russias, was particularly fond of the very strong beer being brewed in London and exported to St Petersburg. One beer was even named in her honour as Imperial Extra Double Stout. These Russian stouts sometimes had a specific gravity as

high as 1.100, producing more than 10% alcohol. They were sold in bottles containing just under one third of a pint and even this much had to be treated with great respect.

The recipe I use is not quite so strong but produces a very fruity beer that still needs long storage. The recipe makes 8 pints.

1kg (2¼ lb) crushed pale malt grains
100g (3½ oz) crystal malt grains
60g (2 oz) black malt
60g (2 oz) wheat flakes
100g (3½ oz) dark brown sugar
30g (1 oz) Fuggles hops

1.25ml (¼ teaspoon) citric acid
4.5 litres (1 gallon) soft water
1.25ml (¼ teaspoon) cooking salt (in hard water areas only)
Stout yeast and nutrient

Heat 4 litres (7 pints) water to 75°C (167°F), pour into an insulated mashing bin, stir in the malts and flakes, the acid and, if necessary, the salt. Cover the bin and maintain a temperature of 65°C (149°F) or just below, for 4 hours.

Strain into a boiling pan, rinse the grains with 575ml (1 pint) of hot water, then discard them. Add all but a handful of the hops, wetting them thoroughly, cover the pan and boil steadily for 1 hour, then leave them to cool in the coldest place available.

Strain through a nylon bag into a fermentation bin, pressing the hops dry. Stir in the sugar, nutrient and an activated yeast. Cover and ferment in a temperature of 17°C (63°F). Skim and stir on the second, third and fourth days, then add the remaining hops and wet them well. Leave the beer well covered to finish fermenting in about another week. Move the bin to a cold place for two days to encourage clarification, then siphon into sixteen half-pint bottles. Prime with caster sugar at the rate of 5ml (1 teaspoon) per 1.2 litres (2 pints). Seal the bottles securely, label them and store in a cool place for one year.

Hydrometer Conversion Tables

Specific gravity	Sugar in 1 gallon	5 litres	Approx. probable % volume of alcohol *after* fermentation
	oz	gram	
1.005	$2\frac{3}{4}$	85	
1.010	$4\frac{3}{4}$	150	0.4
1.015	7	220	1.2
1.020	9	285	2.0
1.025	11	350	2.8
1.030	$13\frac{1}{4}$	415	3.6
1.035	$15\frac{1}{2}$	485	4.3
1.040	$17\frac{1}{2}$	550	5.1
1.045	$19\frac{1}{2}$	615	5.8
1.050	$21\frac{1}{2}$	680	6.5
1.055	$23\frac{3}{4}$	745	7.2
1.060	$25\frac{3}{4}$	810	7.9
1.065	$27\frac{3}{4}$	875	8.6
1.070	30	945	9.3
1.075	32	1010	10.0
1.080	$34\frac{1}{2}$	1075	10.6
1.085	$36\frac{1}{2}$	1140	11.3
1.090	$38\frac{1}{2}$	1205	12.0
1.095	$40\frac{3}{4}$	1275	12.7
1.100	$42\frac{3}{4}$	1340	13.4
1.105	$44\frac{3}{4}$	1405	14.2
1.110	47	1475	14.9
1.115	49	1540	15.6
1.120	$51\frac{1}{4}$	1605	16.3
1.125	$53\frac{1}{4}$	1675	17.1
1.130	$55\frac{1}{2}$	1740	17.8

Note: 1 kg sugar increases the volume of a liquid by 0.62 litre.
2 lb sugar increases the volume of a liquid by 1 pint.

The specific gravity figures in the table are taken at a temperature of 15°C (59°F). If the temperature of the liquid is higher, some adjustment must be made to the last figure of the specific gravity reading.

Temperature of liquid	Addition to last figure of specific gravity
20°C (68°F)	0.9
25°C (77°F)	2.0
30°C (86°F)	3.4
35°C (95°F)	5.0
40°C (104°F)	5.8

Acknowledgments

E. T. Archive: 14 (above), 15, 19 (both), 24, 25 (both), 29 (both), 30, 35 (both), 37, 38, 39 (below), 41 (above), 46 (both), 47, 51 (above), 54, 57 (above), 60, 62 (above), 63, 66, 68 (above), 73 (above), 75

Jean-Loup Charmet: 5, 57 (below), 63, 65, 73 (below), 74, 79

Crown Copyright: 21

Michael Holford: 36

The Library, Royal Botanic Gardens, Kew (photography by Eileen Tweedy): half title, 17, 20, 22, 26, 33, 49, 50 (both), 52, 53, 56, 59, 61, 69, 71, 77

City of Manchester Art Galleries: title page

The Mansell Collection: 62 (below), 78

Museum of English Rural Life, University of Reading: 39 (above), 72

Österreichische Nationalbibliothek, Vienna: 43

Sotheby's Belgravia: front cover, 14 (below), 27, 31, 32, 34, 41 (below), 45, 51 (below), 58, 68 (below)

The Tate Gallery: back cover

Whitecross Studios (John Cook): 6, 8 (both), 10 (both), 13

Glossary

Acid: The cornerstone of bouquet and flavour in wine. Fruits mostly contain citric acid, malic acid or tartaric acid. The quantity varies with the fruit and the season. Some fruits, eg bananas, dates and figs, have virtually none. The recipes indicate the quantity to use.

Adjuncts: Cereals added to malts in the making of beer. They vary the flavour and provide a little extra alcohol. The most popular are flaked maize and flaked rice.

Airlock: A device filled with a sulphite solution, used to seal a fermentation jar. It enables the gas produced during fermentation to escape, but prevents air from getting in.

Campden tablet: The trade name for sodium metabisulphite. It is a strong but safe bactericide and anti-oxidant, especially when mixed with citric acid in water. Widely used as a preservative and preventer of browning – oxidation.

Carbon dioxide: A colourless, tasteless and harmless gas given-off during fermentation.

Demijohn: A clear glass jar with a narrow neck and a nominal capacity of 1 gallon. Widely used both for the fermenting and storage of wines, meads and ciders.

Dry: A lack of sweetness in a wine or beer. The opposite of sweet.

Fermentation: The action of yeast in converting fruit sugars into alcohol and carbon dioxide.

Fermentation-on-the-pulp: Fermenting the fruit juice or sugars in the presence of the crushed fruit.

Ferment-on: Continuing the fermentation after the pulp has been strained out and discarded; also after extra sugar has been added.

Ferment-out: Continuing the fermentation until the yeast has converted all the sugar to alcohol and carbon dioxide or has created so much alcohol that it is prevented from creating more – the end of fermentation.

Fine: The addition of an agent to a wine or beer that coagulates the suspended particles and takes them to the bottom of the container, leaving the wine or beer bright and clear.

Hardening salts: A combination of mineral salts – mainly calcium sulphate and magnesium sulphate – added to soft water that is to be used for making bitter-style beers.

Hops: The dried flower of the vine *Humulus lupulus* used for flavouring beers. Different varieties are used for the different beer styles.

Hydrometer: A simple instrument, like a thermometer in appearance, used in homebrew for measuring the quantity of sugar in a liquid.

Malt: Derived from the barley seed and the basic ingredient of beer. It may be used as a crushed grain, as a toffee-like syrup or as a flour.

Mash: The extraction of the fermentable sugar, maltose, from malt grains by soaking them in hot water for several hours.

Mature: After a wine or beer has been made it needs to rest for a period of time while it reaches the level at which it tastes best.

Metric measures: In the recipes the metric measures are not direct equivalents of Imperial measures. Use metric or Imperial but *not* a combination of both.

Must: A watery liquid containing fruit acids and sugars as well as fruit, vegetable, flower, leaf, herb, cereal or spice essences or pulp before the yeast is added to begin the process of fermentation into wine.

Nutrient: Mineral salts containing nitrogen required by yeast during the fermentation process.

Pectic enzyme: A white powder or brown liquid added to a fruit must to break down the pectin. This aids juice extraction and improves clarification.

Potassium sorbate: A mineral salt used in conjunction with sulphite to terminate fermentation. Sometimes called a wine stabiliser.

Prime: The addition of a small quantity of sugar to a wine, beer, mead or cider to cause a bottle fermentation that gives vitality and a sparkle to the beverage.

Rack: The process of removing clear or clearing wine or beer from its sediment. Often performed with the aid of a siphon.

Rouse: The stirring up of a wort after skimming off the surplus yeast head during fermentation. Air containing oxygen is admitted and enables the yeast to multiply.

Sediment: Particles of pulp and yeast cells, etc., that settle on the bottom of a container after fermentation of wine or beer. If not soon removed it imparts a foul smell and taste to the beverage.

Specific gravity: The weight of a given volume of a liquid compared with the same volume of water at 15°C (59°F). In homebrew the weight is mostly sugar and can be measured with a hydrometer.

Sulphite solution: Water in which sodium metabisulphite is dissolved. Used for sterilising equipment and ingredients. See Campden tablet.

Tannin: A bitter substance found in grape skins, pips and stalks and some other fruits, and added to a must to improve its character.

Topping-up: The addition of a similar wine or water usually to a storage vessel to keep the jar full and so exclude air which would cause deterioration. Sometimes water is added to a fermenting must after the removal of fruit pulp and the stirring in of sugar, to fill up the jar.

Wort: A solution of malt sugars and hop oils and essences before the yeast is added to begin the process of fermentation into beer.

Yeast: A microscopic organism that secretes a number of enzymes that cause the conversion of sugar into alcohol and carbon dioxide. Beer yeast has the name *Saccharomyces cerevisiae.* Wine yeast is a sub-variety called *s.cerevisiae elipsoideus.* There are numerous strains of this, some of which are especially suitable for sweet wines (Sauternes style), dessert wines (Port style), apéritifs (Sherry style), table wines (Hocks, Chablis, Burgundy, Bordeaux styles), and sparkling wines (Champagne style). An All-purpose strain may be used instead if you so wish.

Index